LESS NICE, MORE YOU

Stop Hiding And Become The Most Bold, Authentic Version Of You Now.

DR. AZIZ GAZIPURA

ALSO BY DR. AZIZ GAZIPURA

Books:

The Solution To Social Anxiety

The Art Of Extraordinary Confidence

Not Nice

On My Own Side

100 Wins in 100 Days

Online Publications:

Shrink For The Shy Guy Podcast

Get More Confidence YouTube Channel

Confidence Training Programs:

Confidence University

The Unstoppable Confidence Mastermind

TABLE OF CONTENTS

INTRODUCTION: HOW LONG?

Have you ever had the feeling that you're "too nice"? Perhaps others have told you this, or you've even told yourself this, especially after an incident where you were too accommodating, forgiving, or passive, and got burned as a result.

Maybe it bothers you that you're so nice and you want to be different, but the alternative seems unclear, threatening, destabilizing, and scary. It might seem like a radical change or departure from how you've lived your life, or how a "good person" is *supposed to live*.

How long have you been so nice? How long have you been worried about fitting in, not upsetting others, and holding yourself back so you don't say the "wrong thing?"

How long has guilt been a regular companion, accompanying you throughout your relationships and life? How often do you feel bad for letting others down, not being patient or kind enough, or loving or generous enough? Do you chronically feel like you're not doing enough, falling short, disappointing others... that you should be more and better than what you are?

For how many years have you been trying to mold yourself into the person you're supposed to be? To fit into the roles and rules that mom, dad, family, friends, teachers, bosses, and all the authorities in your life insisted were the right and only way to be?

I invite you to take a moment now and actually think about this. These aren't rhetorical questions. I'm actually curious.

When I ask clients these questions they'll often laugh or chuckle and say something like, "For thirty years", or "My whole life!"

I don't laugh when they tell me. Because I know there's no humor in this and their laugh has nothing to do with mirth or joy. The laugh is more of a cough, an irresistible expression of emotion communicating an immense amount of pain.

The pain of a life not fully lived. The pain of missed opportunities. And perhaps, most severe, the pain of not living as who you are.

Australian palliative care nurse Bronnie Ware spent years working with patients as they lay on their deathbeds. She began interviewing them and uncovering their final regrets, and in doing so, discovered the number one regret people experienced as they approached the hour of their death.

Take a moment to guess right now... what do you imagine it was?

Mistakes they've made or mean things they said? Spending too much time working? Fighting with family and not reuniting quickly enough?

These are all potential regrets, but these are not reflective of the number one regret. That's reserved for a unique form of pain, one that you might be familiar with. The number one regret of the dying is:

"I wish I'd had the courage to live a life true to myself, not the life others expected of me."

In other words, "I lived a life that was not my own."

This can also manifest as, "I was trying to *be somebody else, for somebody else*" Or "I was trying to be the good son, or daughter; the good husband, wife, employee, boss, student." Or "I was doing what I thought I should be doing, being who I was 'supposed' to be."

Are you being who you're supposed to be? Following all of your internal rules to be a "good person" yet feeling more disconnected, disrespected, and ignored as each month passes? As this good person who's doing all the right things, are you feeling more and more tired, burnt out, frustrated, or emotionally flat?

Perhaps you've been aware of this for a while. You might have even acknowledged to yourself and others, saying "Yeah, I'm too nice sometimes." But this way of being seems like the right way to be. It's the only way you've known for so many years. It's who you're *supposed* to be... right?

That, my friend, is insanity. Being something other than who you are, who you're meant to be, so you can conform to someone else's preferences and not make them uncomfortable? Following rules that are not your own so you can satisfy an invisible, internal referee or judge? Sacrificing yourself and your future, not fully living this precious gift of a life, only to discover it as you die with regret on your deathbed?

Yikes. That's brutal.

And, fortunately, that's not how it has to be. That doesn't have to be your destiny. Because you picked up this book, which is a big step in changing the trajectory you're on.

As you read, you will clearly see what I call **The Cage**, which are all the invisible forces that confine you. This Cage is made up of all the rules you've picked up, the roles you're supposed to play, and all the ideas about how you should be. Any aspect of this Cage that doesn't serve you, confines you, or removes you from your true self must go.

We're going to slice through that structure, cut through those walls and have you escape out the side. Or maybe just dynamite that sucker and let the whole thing crumble to rubble so you can emerge from the ashes like a phoenix reborn — fresh, vital, raw, and alive.

Because here's the truth: this isn't just for you. The world needs you.

I know, this might sound like a line from a cheesy superhero movie that makes you roll your eyes. You might question: *who am I? I'm nobody special.* And sure, from a cosmic or geological perspective, you and I aren't that significant. The galaxy twirls, planets orbit, and the sun burns. From that scale what you or I do in our little lifetimes might not matter all that much.

But you are alive here and now. You have been given this life at this time for some reason. You do matter.

The era we're living in has a rate of change that is mind-boggling. Humans are steering a speedboat into uncharted waters at a breakneck pace, and the future of our species is being determined one day at a time.

While you or I might not single-handedly steer the fate of nations or world economies, you do steer the fate of your own life. How you show up today and tomorrow matters. You do have an impact on people around you — your family, friends, spouse, and children. You impact your colleagues, coworkers, employees, clients, and customers. You impact people in the broader communities that you are a part of. In short, you matter.

You are going to be a significant factor in the direction of many people's lives, perhaps many more people than you'll ever realize.

Of course, this is only true if you bust out of that cage of niceness, people-pleasing, hesitation, and holding back. Escape the trap of being who you think you're supposed to be to please others, fit in, and not rock any boats, living a life that is not your own.

You're not here to submissively conform to an invisible cultural field, hiding your true feelings, thoughts, and desires to safely make it through life. The purpose of your life is not to safely make it to the grave without upsetting anyone.

You are meant for more. And the life that you're meant to live, the gifts that you're meant to give, and the people you're meant to touch, will not happen by default. By default, you'll live someone else's life, cautiously letting 10% of the real you out while keeping 90% hidden behind a social mask to please everyone else.

Fuck that!

The time for hiding is done.

The time for people-pleasing, avoidance, and cowardice is done.

The time to cling to your comfort zone behind excuses and stories that you've repeated hundreds of times is done.

The time to step up is now. The time to be 100%, unapologetically YOU is now.

You are ready. The world is waiting.

Dr. Aziz Gazipura

Corbett, Oregon

2023

AUTHOR'S NOTE:

A s you may know, I also wrote a book called "Not Nice: *Stop People Pleasing, Staying Silent, & Feeling Guilty... And Start Speaking Up, Saying No, Asking Boldly, And Unapologetically Being Yourself.*"

You may be wondering what the difference is between that book and this book. I'll quickly explain now.

You can think of "Not Nice" as the textbook on the subject. If you are interested in discovering the depths of your nice training, the hidden sources of your fears of conflict, the relationship between excessive niceness and physical problems and chronic pain, as well as extremely thorough examples of how to speak up and what to say, then Not Nice is a fantastic textbook to study.

This, on the other hand, is not a textbook. It's a lightning bolt. It's intended to activate you, energize you, galvanize you into massive action now. You're picking up this book because you already know you're too nice and it's severely limiting you and your happiness in this life. You don't need to be convinced. You're ready to change things yesterday.

And you know that more study, more insight, more awareness *might* be helpful. But all too often, it doesn't lead to radical and rapid transformation and that's what this book is about.

I want this lightning bolt to strike ground, to jolt you, to shock you into making the changes you need to make *now*. To start a fire that burns away all the structures that you live under that are not your own creation, that confine you and keep you from yourself.

Let's set ablaze anything that is not you.

NOTE: For additional resources, bonuses, and a free mini-course called 3 Steps To Bold Authenticity, go to www.lessnicebook.com

PART I

WHY NICE
ISN'T SO NICE

CHAPTER 1

KIND VS NICE

"Being nice is a good thing…"

"Our world is so messed up because too many people are not nice enough."

"So if everyone becomes selfish that's going to make things better?"

These are just a taste of the thousands of comments and questions I've gotten since challenging that we should all be nice. These challenges arise because many people think the word "nice" is synonymous with being "kind, caring, loving, and sympathetic."

But is it?

According to the Merriam-Webster dictionary, nice means "polite" or "kind." So far so good. At least, that's with the first definition. Just underneath that, nice is defined as: pleasing, agreeable, and appropriate.

Appropriate, eh? According to who's rules?

Being pleasing and agreeable might be a kind thing to do... For example, let's say you're talking with your sweetheart and his or her breath is hard to handle. Do you say something there? If you endure the conversation, trying to breathe through your mouth, is that kind? Is it honest?

What if you said, "Hey sweetie, your breath is pretty strong. Can you brush your teeth and then we can keep talking?" Less of a nice response there. But is that kind? What's the difference?

Kindness involves care and compassion for others. You're aware of their feelings, and you do what you can do to treat others with respect and empathy. Kindness may lead you to do something for someone, even if it has a cost of time, money, or energy for you. Kindness may involve speaking up and telling the truth, even if it temporarily hurts someone's feelings. Or it might involve biting your tongue and letting something slide because you are choosing to be more patient or see the big picture.

Niceness, on the other hand, is actually quite different. In fact, in most if not all cases, niceness is not truly about kindness. There might be a little kindness in there, but it's much lower down on the list of priorities. When it comes to niceness, priority number one is about keeping everyone's feelings smooth. It comes from the need to make sure no one feels hurt, upset, angry, disappointed, disliked, rejected, sad, or any other "negative" emotion. In short, niceness means you don't "make others feel bad."

Most of us learned that the best way to not make others feel bad is to avoid disagreement, conflict, saying no, asking for what you want, having different opinions, or challenging others in any way. In other words, just be a submissive extension of other people's will and desires.

"But wait," you may ask, "isn't that the golden rule? And shouldn't that be a rule to live by — don't make others feel bad?"

On the surface, this approach to life holds some value. The other day our kids came home from school talking about how another kid in their class is a "fatty." We had a discussion about how singling someone out for being different and calling them names about it can cause a lot of pain.

In fact, my wife, Candace, shared this heart-breaking story of being on the school bus when she was six years old, where all the kids picked on a girl because she smelled bad. No one wanted to sit next to her and they all criticized and mocked her. One day, there were no seats open, and Candace had to sit next to this girl. As soon as she sat down, she turned towards the girl and said, "You smell like pee." The girl turned towards Candace with a pleading look in her eyes and said, "I can't help it. I have a medical problem."

Candace felt heartbroken, feeling waves of empathy rocket through her six year old nervous system as she made eye contact with this poor, little, stinky girl. She said it changed her in a deep way and reminded her that we don't really know what's going on for people. Me and my boys sat entranced as my wife finished her story. Lesson transmitted.

But is that the end of the story? Is there any nuance about when or how to speak up? Niceness removes all nuance and creates general commandments, such as "Don't speak up" and "Don't be selfish."

With just a few probing questions, the whole "Just be nice" philosophy starts to reveal some huge gaps. Do you actually

"make" others feel bad? What if someone already feels bad —
is it your job to avoid certain topics and try to make them feel
better? What if you don't know what will "make" someone
feel bad — should you just play it safe and avoid most topics?

What if saying what feels true to you causes temporary
upset in someone else? What if doing something that feels
important to you leads to someone else being upset or judging
you? In other words, what if your being honest or authentic
leads to upsetting someone else?

One client of mine who was following the "Just be nice and
don't upset others" approach to life stayed in a dysfunctional
marriage for fifteen years. He knew his relationship wasn't
working for him for over a decade, but if he brought up any
challenges, his partner would start to cry and withdraw. So
he held his tongue, settled, and endured in order to be nice,
as his vitality and happiness dwindled away.

This is where being nice as a life philosophy and a social
survival strategy starts to break down. For the thousands of
excessively nice people I've worked with over the last two
decades, if being real caused upset, or even *could* cause upset,
then it was off the table as an option.

And yet, you, I, and most people do value kindness,
tolerance, treating others with respect, and generally, trying
to be kind to our brothers and sisters on this planet. Below
are four distinct ways true kindness is very different from
niceness. This distinction is important to cover right at the start
of this book, because as long as you think being nice equals
being a kind, "good" person, then your old programming
will stop you from changing even before you've started. Let
this list below clear the way and relieve you of any confusion.

1. Kindness is real and authentic. Niceness is fake and forced.

Kindness involves caring for people, including yourself. But if anything you're doing involves saying things that you don't believe, suppressing your actual desires and perspectives, and otherwise hiding the truth so as to not upset anyone, then it is certainly not kind to yourself. This is niceness, and it has forced quality to it, as you are effortfully constructing an image of a kind person, although inside you don't necessarily think or believe what you are representing.

2. Kindness is a choice. Niceness is a compulsion.

Someone can choose to be supportive and generous with another. You can also choose to offer less support in that moment if you feel lower in resources or otherwise not inspired to give in that way.

With niceness, however, there is no choice. If someone needs something, you have a compulsive need to give it. Your desires, other commitments, or well-being are irrelevant. It's selfish and mean to prioritize yourself and your wants or needs. Just do whatever is needed at the moment, as it's the "good" and "right" thing to do, or so the nice story goes.

3. Kindness leaves a glow of joy in the giver. Niceness leaves a residue of resentment.

When you act with true kindness, you feel good from connecting and giving to others. Maybe you skipped a meal to stay longer for a friend, or missed an evening out to take care of your mom. But when these gifts are given freely, you feel a sense of satisfaction in taking care of others, sharing, supporting, and loving through your actions.

Giving from a place of niceness often is tainted by feelings of obligation, burden, and "I have to or else…" This means the source of motivation is fear rather than love, and a part of you resists this forced action. It doesn't matter whether you feel up to it or not, just give. And then give more.

This kind of fearful and pressured giving creates tension, agitates the fight/flight response in the nervous system, and leads to resentment. Of course, if you're really nice, you don't consciously feel resentment either. You just feel drained, irritated, anxious, depressed, or mysteriously foggy and fatigued.

4. Kindness is focused on supporting others. Niceness is focused on self-survival.

Kindness is born out of an innate human desire to connect with and contribute to others. We are pack creatures and possess many millennia of evolutionary programming to want to give to and support our fellow humans. When coming from kindness, you are truly curious about what those around you need and focus your attention on helping them realize it.

Niceness is less about the other person and more about you. Indeed, you do want the other person to get what they want, but primarily because you want to feel better. Because if they are upset or suffering in any way, you feel anxious and unsettled. You mainly want the other person's bad feelings to go away, so you can return to a sense of safety and normalcy.

As you can see, upon a closer look, kindness and niceness are actually very different qualities. Now let's clarify exactly what niceness really is.

CHAPTER 2

NICENESS IN A NUTSHELL

So, if niceness isn't the same thing as kindness, what exactly is it? At its core, niceness is a survival strategy that follows this logic: *if I can fit into the group and not stand out in any negative way, I'll be safe and survive. I must not say or do anything that challenges the cultural norms of the group, or else others will be upset and reject me. This disapproval will lead to fewer opportunities, exclusion, or even exile from the group, and if that happens, I won't be able to survive.*

A particularly savvy or emotionally intelligent nice person will take this one step beyond mere disapproval avoidance and will actually become very proactive in seeking others' approval. In this case, the logic is: *if I don't upset you and treat you with extra respect, deference, warmth, care, special treatment, agreeableness, and enthusiastic positive regard, then I will maximize my chances of you liking me back.*

This survival strategy expands to become an entire philosophy, personality, identity and way of life. Thus, the nice person isn't aware they are merely running a survival strategy. They only consciously know that they must behave this way in order to be a "good person." They know that if they maintain this status of a good person in the eyes of others, then their relationships will be okay, life will be okay, and I will be okay (aka, safe).

This life philosophy may even extend beyond human relations and expand into the spiritual dimension. If I'm a good person, then good things will come to me via karma, God's grace, and so forth. In other words, if you please not only your fellow humans, but the divine forces of creation, then you certainly will have a smooth life filled with ease, goodies, and (most importantly), safety and protection from harm.

If you were to do something that was not nice, then that would not be the actions of a good person. That's very bad, of course. Even if no one else saw you or knew it, you'd be wracked with guilt if you were to do something that would put you into this category of a bad person. As a result, you work very hard to be vigilant, police yourself, and do your best to be good.

As you read this, you might question what the problem is... *aren't we just talking about a conscience here? Of course, I want to be a good person who does good things. Of course, I feel guilty when I fall short of this.*

Actually, niceness differs quite a bit from a true conscience, sense of integrity, or personal code of ethics. In true integrity, you have values and rules you attempt to live by, because it feels right to you. You may value patience or kindness, so you attempt to embody that with your kids or aging parents.

Your values may lead you to challenge others, such as speaking up if you see deceit or misuse of power because you value protecting others. Maybe you speak the truth in a close relationship because you value honesty and true intimacy, even if it leads to temporary turbulence or friction.

Niceness, on the other hand, does not follow a code of personal ethics. In niceness, your values are largely absent. Because the rules you attempt to follow are the default rules you absorbed from the culture in which you were raised. You have an extensive list of all the rules about how you "should be" that you learned from mom, dad, teachers, peers, religious groups, and the popular media. This list of rules is often conflicting, unrealistic, and dominated by one overarching rule: don't upset anyone.

Hence, you might actually bend over backward, deny yourself, tolerate mistreatment, or break your own real values in order to please, placate, or otherwise preserve a relationship.

Have you ever done this? How did it feel to do this? Most likely, not great.

In sum, niceness is a survival strategy designed to keep you safe by avoiding disapproval. It's not necessarily bad or wrong. It's just an attempt to survive. Rather than it being sinister, it's really just scared.

CHAPTER 3

THE PLIGHT OF THE PLEASER

One synonym people use for niceness is the term "people pleaser." At first glance, being a pleaser doesn't sound so bad, does it? I mean, it's good to please your customers, right? Isn't it good if a husband wants to please his wife, or vice versa?

It almost sounds loving or respectful to desire to please people. After all, the definition of please is to "give pleasure or satisfaction." That sure sounds like a loving thing to do.

Yet this may be another euphemism designed to make us feel better, or look better, even though what we're doing is very different.

Let's look at a few common examples of people-pleasing to see what's really going on here.

Ted works in a large company with lots of collaborative meetings. These meetings involve frequently sharing ideas without clear direction, and they often drag on. Ted feels bored and disengaged, and thinks many of the ideas shared are not actually practical or useful. He tells himself that he's being too judgmental, that this is how big companies work, and to just stay silent and get through the meetings the best he can.

Hannah wants more of her partner's attention. When he comes home from work, he's often preoccupied and silent. When Hannah shares the details of her day, he seems distracted and restless, and doesn't ask any questions or seem that curious about her. He then shares a lot about his struggles at work and expects Hannah to listen to and support him. She tells herself that he's going through a stressful time and needs her support right now and that she's being too needy for wanting more.

Teressa's roommate borrows her clothing and other items, often without asking. Teressa has brought it up in the past, telling her roommate that this bothers her and she prefers that she ask her before borrowing something. Her roommate sometimes asks, but often still does not. Further still, if her roommate asks, Teressa instantly says "Yes," whether she wants to lend the items or not, telling herself that saying no would be rude or selfish if she wasn't going to wear the clothes that day.

Here are three different situations in which people might have something to say but they don't fully speak up. In each circumstance, they have a number of thoughts that prevent them from speaking up more directly. These thoughts judge them for being too sensitive, needy, selfish, etc. and claim that not speaking up is for the benefit of the other people involved. It will please them.

But what's really going on here? These three situations, and another three thousand pleasing scenarios all boil down to one simple purpose: to avoid discomfort. Ted, Hannah, and Teressa are avoiding speaking up, not because they are kind, patient, or "good" people... They are not speaking up because they're scared.

They're scared of the discomfort of the interactions, and more specifically, they're scared of the emotional discomfort they will feel if someone else gets upset. Hence, people-pleasing — which is just another phrase for "being nice" — is a fearful pattern of avoidance. Avoidance of assertiveness, speaking your perspective, sharing your feelings, and direct contact with others. Avoidance of authenticity and real connection.

Like all avoidance tactics, the longer you avoid, the harder it becomes to stop avoiding. Avoiding what you're scared of tends to magnify the sense of danger, amplify your fear, and weaken your ability to confront the issue effectively, as you aren't practicing and building your capacities.

To put it even more directly, people-pleasing is cowardice — it's a refusal to take your life into your hands and steer. When pleasing, you're saying, "Who do you want me to be?" and then carrying out those orders.

A key question to ask is, who is the "you" that is determining how you're supposed to be? It could be your colleagues, boss, or friends. It could be your partner, spouse, or parents. It could even be someone you just met on a first date, a neighbor you barely know, or a stranger at a restaurant or bar. That person now determines how you should behave. A stranger decides your destiny.

Thus is the plight of the pleaser. A life in which your unique expression is heavily filtered so as to conform to the desires of everyone else. You mold yourself to fit the circumstance so that no one could possibly get upset. You contort to whatever shape is needed to avoid the disapproval of others, which might even mean enabling their dysfunctional patterns.

Just keep your head down and do your work, Ted. Just put a smile on your face, be patient, and listen endlessly to your husband, Hannah. Stop being so difficult, Teressa; just let your roommate borrow your clothes. You weren't even going to wear that outfit today anyway. It doesn't matter what you want , feel, or perceive. Just do what others want, as this is what makes you a "good" person.

Sure, with all this avoiding, suppressing, and filtering, you're not really being you, not really living your life. But at least you're being "good," right? That's gotta count for something...

CHAPTER 4

ROLE SUFFOCATION

If this is all sounding very familiar to you, and you're realizing that you have adopted the nice person survival strategy, know that you did so for one reason: at one point in your life, you needed to do so.

Perhaps you were in a threatening, unstable, or abusive environment. Or maybe your parents and surrounding community exerted strong pressure on you to be a certain way and indeed, would reject or exile you if you didn't obey. It may have been even more subtle than this, and you simply were a sensitive child who strongly felt the emotions of those around you and began adapting your behavior to minimize their discomfort. Regardless of the exact origins, at one point in your life, it seemed like your survival was at stake.

However, at this point in your life, that survival strategy is no longer necessary and certainly doesn't serve you in the highest sense. In other words, it's time for an update. You'll discover soon how to radically upgrade your approach to life, but first, you need to understand how you've been playing the game up until this point.

Way back when, when you were growing up as a young human, you looked to parents, peers, and the culture at large to determine how you "should" be to receive approval and acceptance. You study this ever-growing list of requirements and create simplistic rules to follow for each role you play in your life.

For example, at home, you learn that a good son does what his parents want quickly and obediently without questioning or hesitation. At school, you learn that an acceptable boy doesn't cry, even when he's hurt. You learn from your pious uncle that a Godly boy does what he is told and obeys the Father, whose commandments are written in the good book.

Each experience expands your list of rules. You didn't learn just one rule about how you should be as a son or daughter. You learned hundreds. You learned hundreds more about how you should be from peers in order to be liked, attractive, popular, desirable, and worthy. Rules pile upon rules, and by the time you are an adult, you have a list so long you can hardly keep track.

Some of your rules may reflect your values. For example, you might value open-mindedness, so you have a rule not to attack someone for having a different viewpoint than yours. Other rules might not reflect your values at all.

Perhaps you have a rule that says you should never interrupt, or always stay silent because challenging someone's opinion makes you pushy, jerky, or argumentative. This rule, and thousands like it, can block you from healthy connections, relationships and self-expression.

So what's the problem with all these rules? It turns out they can be extremely limiting, confining, painful, and ultimately not you. Instead of authenticity and purpose guiding your life, you're being steered by a tremendous fear of not fitting into these roles, and hence, you're following the rules of each role to the tee. Part of you believes *if I'm not playing this role well by following all the rules, then I won't be loved, I'll lose all respect from others, and I'll be rejected, shunned, and hurt.*

You might experience a disproportionate amount of shame and fear when you don't live up to the rules of one of your roles. A vague, creeping sense of dread can overtake you. A feeling of shame, horribleness, badness, and an irrational fear of being harshly rejected or abandoned may arise out of seemingly nowhere.

I noticed this in myself just the other night. My wife, Candace, seemed upset at bedtime. With all the chaos of trying to get two young wild boys to sleep, we didn't have a chance to talk more, and I fell asleep without knowing what she was experiencing. She could be upset for 1,001 different reasons, most of which have nothing to do with me or what I have or haven't done. Even if she were upset with me, we have hundreds of difficult conversations under our belt, and I know we can work through anything. We're in this to win it. In for life, no matter what.

Yet, I woke up the next morning feeling anxious. My mind created a story that she was upset with me, and that I was letting her down in some way, and that ultimately, after being disappointed for years, she would leave me. This story exists despite us having a truly beautiful and extraordinary relationship, lives that are deeply intertwined, and no indication whatsoever of her having major grievances that would warrant leaving.

Can you relate? Have you ever had an irrational fear of being left by a partner or something bad happening in your workplace or other relationships? What's going on here?

When that dread occurs, it's a signal that you're breaking some of the rules in one or more of your roles. Later that morning, I had some time to reflect and uncover several rules I had not been consciously aware of. I discovered that in the role of husband, one of my rules is to please my wife and ensure she is always happy. If she is upset, disappointed, angry, or sad, then she is obviously not pleased. I must do everything in my power to "fix" her emotions and make her pleased. If my wife is not pleased, then pain, danger, abandonment, and ruin await.

It turns out this is an exceedingly common rule in romantic relationships. Fortunately, most of the time, I am not under the spell of these old rules. I spend most of my life securely attached to Candace, feeling love and trust. But this wasn't always the case. I spent decades completely controlled by the rules within my roles, chronically feeling unlovable, unworthy, and disappointing to others. Hence the occasional bouts of anxiety, arising from the echoes of the past.

What are the major roles you play in your life right now? Are you a husband or wife? Mother or father? Son or daughter? Brother or sister? Man or woman? Friend? Boss? Employee? Doctor, lawyer, mechanic, programmer, engineer?

Have you also adopted other roles such as the "funny, playful person" who's always upbeat, or "the saint" who is full of endless compassion, or "the smart person" who must always know everything or have an answer.

Pick three of the biggest roles you identify with right now. Perhaps it's your gender, a role in your family, or a title at work. For each one, write out a list of some of the rules that come to your mind. Don't overthink this, or spend hours coming up with a comprehensive list. Some rules might be obvious; some might take a few minutes to uncover, and some might seem like they reflect your values, and some are clearly bat sh*t crazy. That's all perfect. Whatever you uncover is good.

And yes, I just introduced an Action Step into this book. Wasn't it super smooth and casual? No big fanfare or special heading; we just rolled right into it. It's best to have a file on your phone or paper journal to do an action step and the other action steps. Don't worry, this book won't have a ton of them, and they won't take you hours on end. Instead, we'll be applying the philosophy of "minimum effective dose" — doing just what is needed to accelerate the change you're undergoing.

Yet, having said that, no true or lasting transformation occurs without action. Reading self-development books without action is just the sophisticated person's entertainment. Action leads to new experiences, which changes you like no reading or reflecting can. Also, action can be uncomfortable, which is the fastest, and only the path to liberation from niceness to the real you.

If you want to go ahead and do this action now, then keep reading. If you don't want to do this, and you don't plan on coming back later to do it, then most likely, you're looking more for insight or a quick-fix rather than total liberation. I reckon you've got more in you, and I bet you want more.

So come on, commit right now to do this action step and the other ones speckled throughout this book. Let's create a life where instead of your number one regret being you didn't live a life that was your own, your number one regret at the end of this crazy ride is that you had so many amazing relationships, connections, adventures, contributions, and experiences that you can't decide which one thing is your favorite.

Allow me to introduce you to Easy Going Aziz, one of [handwritten: Easy Going David] the roles I play. Easy Going Aziz is patient, loving, flexible, adaptable, low needs, and easy to get along with. He's kind and non-judgmental too.

Do I embody those qualities? Sure… sometimes. Sometimes, I naturally am this way. Sometimes I'm faking it. When I'm faking it, I will smile when I don't want to, nod when I don't really agree, avoid saying what I really think or feel, ask questions instead of sharing directly, and will tend to be neutral and say vague things.

At the same time, I feel a strong desire to get the hell out of there, and yet, I feel bound to stay in the conversation, continuing to give the appearance of a calm, non-judgmental presence, which is actually full of secret judgments that I'm just not saying.

Then I leave feeling tense, agitated, drained, and resentful, replaying many moments of the conversation. Part of me is angry that I forced myself to do that and I feel disgusted by the inauthenticity, by playing a role that is false, by being fake. Another part of me is angry at the other person, judging them harshly. And still, another part is relentlessly judging me for having judgments, for feeling aversion, for wanting to get out of there.

Do you have those parts too? [handwritten: YES] The judging part is doing everything it can — judging, condemning, and shaming — to keep you within that role. Oh my, how effective it is. For a long time it's worked, suppressing you, suffocating the real you.

Until now.

CHAPTER 5

BACKGROUND RADIATION

A ll these roles with all their rules make it quite hard for you to simply relax and enjoy yourself. This is why so many nice people experience anxiety, bad moods, and physical ailments and illnesses. Their bodies are chronically aroused in a stress state, perpetually tense and on-guard for the danger of falling short of one of their hundreds, or even thousands, of rules.

This list of 700 ways you could fall short and be in danger creates what I call the "background radiation." Why that term? Because I'm secretly a space nerd. In the 1940's, an even bigger space nerd than me, the American cosmologist Ralph Apher, predicted our entire universe should have something he called the "Cosmic Microwave Background."

He figured that if there was a "big bang" in which all energy exploded out from a single point, then the original energy from this explosion should be way out there in space somewhere. About 20 years later, two researchers working at Bell Telephone were creating a radio receiver and picked up "noise" uniformly from all over the sky. It turns out they'd discovered background radiation. It's everywhere, all at once, in all directions. They found that you just can't see it or "hear" it without the right instruments.[1]

The tension created from internal pressure to follow all your self-imposed rules and the persistent fear this creates makes up your own personal "background radiation." It leads to a sense of unease that you're not doing it right, whatever "it" is. Perhaps it's life, or your relationships, job, fitness, or anything really; You're not properly fulfilling all your roles and obeying all the rules; you're not doing enough, and you're bound to let others down. Basically, something, somewhere, is going wrong, or it will soon, so look out.

Much like those researchers at the Bell labs, you can actually tune into this background radiation and listen to it. It requires you to slow down, turn off all screens, audios and videos, turn off even more screens, your smart fridge, and be in silence. Breath. Focus on your body and notice what is happening now. Do you feel any sort of unease, restlessness, agitation, or tension? Do your chest or ribs feel tight? Is your jaw or stomach tense? Let yourself slow down even more and feel, inviting all of these sensations to just be there. Become curious and listen, and you will start to hear the background radiation.

What do you hear? When I tune into the background radiation, I'll observe thoughts like:

- I need to give and do more for Candace; I'm letting her down.
- I should be working more and earning more.

---

1 https://www.space.com/33892-cosmic-microwave-background.html

- I have to make sure nothing goes wrong with anything in our house.

- I worked too much this week, my boys are missing me.

- I don't wrestle with them enough; a father should wrestle with his boys every time they want to.

- I should be doing more for all of my clients. I'm letting everyone down.

- I should respond to friends and family faster and reach out to them more often (my mind then cycles through people I haven't followed up with in a while, creating a sense of unease, guilt, and general "badness").

We respond to this noise in various ways. First, it creates a chronic tension and stress response, which can create physical pain in any system in your body, from your muscles, to your tendons, to your organs. These pains are often unsolvable in the traditional "cut it out or fix it with chemicals" approach to medicine. They often move from one body part to another and get placed in bucket diagnosis categories like irritable bowel syndrome, chronic fatigue syndrome, tendonitis, or fibromyalgia.[2]

Furthermore, we often make a number of decisions based on the whispers of this background noise, without even consciously being aware of this influence. From the list above, I may snuggle Candace, change my work schedule, wrestle with my boys, make numerous phone calls to friends or family, and go above and beyond the promises of my coaching programs to give more time, all without even checking with

---

2 For a deeper look into how niceness can create pain, see Chapter XX of Not Nice. You can also go straight to the source and read The Way Out by Alan Gordon or Think Away Your Pain by David Schecter MD.

myself to see if that's really needed, what I actually want to do, or feel like I have the resources for.

In other words, **you might make automatic, unconscious decisions to follow certain rules that** *you don't even know you have.* Over time, this lack of awareness and the choices that result can pull you further and further from yourself, leading to the third consequence of the background radiation: inauthenticity.

At first glance, that one doesn't sound nearly as bad as painful guts and migraine headaches, does it? But unfortunately, it's still pretty bad I'm afraid. Because carrying out your life by not really being yourself is possibly the greatest pain of all. Sure, it might not hit you between the eyes like a ton of bricks as a migraine would, or bring you to your knees like a spasm in your lower back. But don't let the subtle nature of it fool you.

Living life on autopilot, unconsciously carrying out the roles, and following all the rules adds up slowly to create your own personal version of hell. You might have a spouse and kids that love you, but you nevertheless feel hollow and empty inside. You may have career success and money but be riddled with anxiety or loneliness or meaninglessness. You may have everything to be grateful for, and yet, you feel frustrated and angry on the inside.

Worse still, not living your life and being chronically oppressed by an endless list of internal rules is not a problem that is really acknowledged anywhere. It's not a symptom of a disorder in the Diagnostic and Statistics Manual that mental health professionals would use to diagnose a psychiatric ailment. Instead, they might call it depression and label it as a "chemical imbalance" (even though this theory has never been supported in research but is rather a marketing angle concocted by pharmaceutical companies[3]), and give you a bottle of pills. "If those pills don't work, come back in three weeks and we'll add some more."

Now you have a diagnosis of Irritable Bowel Syndrome, Chronic Fatigue Syndrome, and persistent migraines. "You can take some meds for those too, if you'd like." Top it off with an SSRI, and maybe throw in an antipsychotic too. "Don't be scared of the name, we use those all the time as an adjunct to the SSRI's. That combo seems to work great. Don't worry about your roles or your rules. These problems are physical and we got a pill for that."

All the while, the background radiation drums on, pulsing in the distance. *Do more, you're not enough, danger, ruin, abandonment, be more, give more, be nicer, don't feel that way, you're bad...*

I wonder what your background radiation is whispering to you?

---

3 To discover more about this, read *The Emperor's New Drugs: Exploding the Antidepressant Myth* by Irving Kirsch.

CHAPTER 6

CONFUSION

"I'm confused," she said. "I just don't know what's right for me."

Amanda had been telling me about some difficulties she'd been experiencing in her dating life. She'd been talking with a man on video calls who lived in a different city. At first, she felt excited to talk, was attracted to him and eager to get on their next call. As some time passed, she found her attraction waning, and even found some of his text messages annoying.

She began our session by telling me how she had a "history of avoiding intimacy" and that she always ran away from getting close to people. Her theory was that she was playing out this same pattern again, and instead of running away, she needed the confidence to keep dating this man.

"Maybe," I said. "Let's investigate."

Secretly, I disagreed with her theory. Not because I had any agenda one way or the other regarding this particular dating partner. I didn't know the guy, and he sounded respectful and attentive. No, my issue came from the little clues I heard Amanda drop as she spoke about the situation.

My first clue was that she said she was "confused" and didn't know what she wanted. In my work with thousands of clients over the years, I have seen that people almost always know more than they first imagine. A storm of confusion churns the surface waters as they bounce around in their minds. But below the surface, the answer for the next step is always clear.

That storm is caused by the background radiation coming to the foreground, creating a disturbance or noise that prevents Amanda from hearing herself. As she enters into dating, her rules become loud and demanding, creating a strong pressure to behave in certain ways.

She revealed in her conversation with me some of her inner desires and her rules, all jumbled together, hence the confusion. She told me that she initially felt attracted to him because he was very attentive, present, and patient. He appreciated her authenticity and desire to be real, and he responded in kind. So far, so good.

"And yet there's a part of you that isn't quite feeling it... What's missing?" I asked her.

"Well..." she took a long pause. "I feel like I have a strong sense of humor, and I like being able to banter and create spontaneous silly characters and play with each other. My humor doesn't seem to fully land for him, and we don't joke around that much... Maybe he's a bit too serious and focused on growth. I mean, I like to grow. But I also like to not be growing all the time and just have fun."

Before I could respond, she continued. "But we haven't met in person yet, just video calls. So how could I know that for sure? He did say he's interested in adventure and having fun, so maybe I'm just not seeing it."

Maybe…

Did you catch that?

It's a pattern I see all the time and know extremely well because I did it myself for decades. It's a ninja level maneuver of self-invalidation. Basically, you have a feeling, sense, or perspective. And then, you immediately question, challenge or dismiss it without even letting yourself fully hear it and sit with it for a few minutes.

Why would someone do that? Why do you imagine Amanda just did that? Why have you in the past?

Because her feelings and perceptions conflict with her rules. Let me explain. She has a pretty clear signal coming from her inner guidance system that's telling her she's not fully satisfied with their resonance when it comes to connecting through humor. To put it more simply, he seems a little too serious and doesn't get her sense of humor.

Hearing that signal fully might make her change course with him. Perhaps she would prefer to be friends instead of dating. Or maybe she'd want to conclude speaking with each other entirely. But, she happens to have a rule that prohibits this. At least, that's my best guess from seeing this play out with so many nice people. So I asked her.

"How would you feel if you imagined telling him that you preferred to be friends instead of dating… or maybe even stopped dating him entirely?"

"Whew," she exhaled. "That would be tough. I'd feel bad. He's so kind and patient with me. I mean he's present and aware and vulnerable. What's wrong with me that I don't feel attracted to a man like that?"

Bingo. More self-invalidation, plus a self-judgment thrown in for good measure. This is definitely her "nice" programming speaking at this point. My guess is there's some rules in there about not hurting other people, that she shouldn't let others down, or once she's connected with someone she's responsible for their feelings.

This is why dating and relationships can be so difficult and borderline impossible for very nice people. If you feel compelled by guilt to ensure people never feel pain because of you, then it's very hard to get close to others. Dating and relationships are high-impact sports. You, those you date, and those you love and form deep relationships with, such as a partner, spouse, or children... all of those people will be hurt at some point in their relationship with you. They will, at times, feel disappointed, unheard, irritated, angry, or upset with you. Just as you will with them.

The nice person's rules of "Don't ever say or do anything that can hurt another person" are rigid, simplistic, and unrealistic attempts to avoid the reality of relationships and life. Real relationships are messy, and there's no way around that.

Because of the noise of all these rules, Amanda couldn't even hear the simple, clear signals coming from her heart and her intuition. Signals like: *I like this, I don't like that.* Basic and primary signals that all of us must receive clearly to successfully steer in this life.

CHAPTER 7
LIKES AND DISLIKES

As a nice person, it's generally not okay to dislike things, especially people. Sure, you can generally dislike some vague concept like, "I don't like inconsiderate people." That's allowed. But in your practical, daily life experience, you're not really allowed to dislike or judge people, are you?

I'm not saying that you *actually* don't dislike or judge anyone. You just do it, and then have to stuff those judgments down, creating a storm of confusion like Amanda did in her dating life.

For years, whenever I noticed myself judging someone or feeling aversion towards someone, I would experience an onslaught of reprimands from my mind telling me it was wrong to judge, that I was being "too judgmental," that I was a hypocrite because I probably did the same kinds of things that I was judging someone else for doing, and on and on.

The more I studied spirituality and psychology, the worse it got. My inner nice police were armed with countless philosophies and theories, from blaming my overactive ego that was feeding on judgment, to labeling it as an unconscious projection of my own flaws.

At the root of all this pressure was a simple rule: *I should not dislike anybody or anything about anybody.* In other words, I shouldn't experience judgmental thoughts or feel aversion towards someone, especially not those that I'm close with.

Do you see how problematic this one rule could be? How this one single rule could completely prevent me from having healthy, real relationships with others? And that's just one! Imagine if you had twenty other such crazy rules bouncing around in there?

I could see a similar rule operating in Amanda. Like and dislike — or attraction and aversion — are the most basic, primary signals we receive throughout the day. Should you have absolutely no food preference and basically like everything the same? Raw broccoli, baby carrots dipped in ranch, burnt toast, a ripe summer peach, or bowl of warm cinnamon oatmeal... who cares? I like them all the same.

How absurd would that be?

What if you couldn't dislike any form of clothing? Would you wear clothing made for any gender, any size, or any style? I imagine your outfits would certainly be quite unique. On the plus side, others might think you were some sort of eccentric genius.

In reality, from a very young age, you develop preferences and are guided by your likes and dislikes. Ask your parents, and I guarantee that they'll tell you which foods you liked and which ones you hated as a kid (and which ones you pretended to eat but spit into your napkin... oh yes, they saw you even though you thought you were being super sneaky).

It turns out the same system is sending those messages of like and dislike to you today. Not just about your food and clothing choices, but also about people, places, environments, and opportunities. Instead of stuffing everything from the aversion side into the "bad" category of judgment, what if you got curious instead?

That's exactly what I did with Amanda. I had her list out the qualities that she found most attractive in a partner. I even encouraged her to not settle for "or," but go for "and." So instead of "I want a man who is present *or* humorous *or* growth-oriented," how about, "I want a partner who is present *and* humorous *and* growth-oriented, *and… AND!*"

It's okay to like what you like and dislike what you dislike. You don't need to heavily overanalyze it or "solve" all your dislikes until you are a placid being who has no preferences.

Besides, your aversion system that tells you it doesn't like things is actually extremely valuable. It might alert you to someone who is clearly *not* a good fit for you. Have you ever overridden that part of you and then gotten into something that was definitely *not* in your best interest? What would happen if you allowed yourself to hear those clear signals and listened to them more?

You do not have to be good.
You do not have to walk on your knees
for a hundred miles through the desert repenting.
You only have to let the soft animal of your body
love what it loves.

— Mary Oliver

CHAPTER 8

INAUTHENTICITY TOLERANCE

If someone's been running the nice survival strategy for decades, and they learned from their family growing up that nice is the best and anything other than nice is selfish and wrong, then most likely they have an identity built up about being a "nice person" (aka, a "good person").

There's almost a bit of pride in it. "I'm one of the good ones. Not one of those selfish, bad, mean people out there in the world." But while you might feel a sense of pride in being nice, you're actually taking a sense of pride in how inauthentic you can be. Because it turns out that extremely nice people have an extremely high inauthenticity tolerance.

Your inauthenticity tolerance is how much you can handle being fake, hiding, pretending, posturing, or suppressing the real you to keep things smooth. If your inauthenticity tolerance is high, then if you feel the impulse to challenge someone, you push it down. Your friend asks you what you think of that restaurant, person or movie, and you will give some sort of vague answer because you don't know how your friend feels and you don't want to disagree with them. A colleague at work overrides you in a meeting and you push down your urge to speak up because you're terrified of conflict.

And on and on you go. Moment after moment. Week after week. Year after year.

Many nice clients I work with historically had an extremely high inauthenticity tolerance. In other words, they sustained the ruse of being a calm, flexible, low-needs, nice person for a very long time. They fooled everyone, including themselves into believing that this is indeed who they really are. All the while, they experience a persistent and ever-increasing sense of anxiety and disconnection.

They feel disconnected because they are. They've veered so far from their real selves and for so long that they have lost sight of who's really in there. I've seen gay clients live the life of heterosexual men so as not to upset family members. I've seen others stay in relationships they know are not healthy or good for them because they don't want to "ruin their kids' lives." I've seen people stay in careers they chose decades ago to please their parents. I'm sure you know people like this as well.

How high is your inauthenticity tolerance?

How many environments can you go to and keep it all down, hidden, and suppressed? Do you do it at work? At home? With family? With friends?

How far has it gone? Have you lost touch with the real you? Is it buried under so many years of rules and pretending that you don't really even know who's there underneath?

Stuffing, suppressing, avoiding, hiding.

Stuffing, suppressing, avoiding, hiding.

It starts to sound like the rhythm of machines at work in a factory. Only this factory isn't producing toys for children. It's producing death for your soul.

How.

Long.

Are.

You.

Going.

To.

Keep.

Stuffing?

This isn't sustainable and you know it. Which is why you're here, reading these words. The time for changing is coming, and coming fast. Because at some point, after decades of suppressing, your capacity to keep it all together, to pretend and suppress will just stop. Then the breakdown will occur. And it will be glorious.

PART II
BREAKING FREE

CHAPTER 9

THE BREAKDOWN

There will come a time when it will all start to fall apart. Perhaps not in a dramatic way that involves flipping over the table, telling your boss to shove it and then quitting your job, or instantly ending a relationship you know you've stayed in way too long for the wrong reasons. While these sorts of things can certainly happen, often, the breakdown begins long before those external actions. It starts when your inauthenticity tolerance begins to plummet. All of a sudden going into that meeting and playing nice, pretending there's no tension or weird dynamics happening seems completely intolerable; being with your friends and dodging certain topics to avoid any potential conflict makes you feel like you're going to explode; not having that raw and real conversation with your partner because you know he or she might get upset feels completely unacceptable.

Even though you may have lived this way for many years, and you know exactly how to play the role just right, doing so seems out of the question. You are shocked at how long you've been under this spell, how others have treated you, how you've *let* others treat you. Like waking from a dream, you see yourself and your life more clearly than ever before.

With that clarity comes one resounding decision: *I'm done. I'm done living this way. I'm unwilling to keep doing this. To keep hiding, holding back, and attempting to please others just so they'll like me.*

With this clarity might come strong feelings of aversion. You might even shake your head in surprise or disgust at all the ways you've tolerated poor treatment, smiled when you wanted to scream, or sacrificed your own perceptions so you could agree with someone that you clearly didn't agree with.

As the breakdown progresses, this aversion grows in intensity. It feels like a fire raging through the underbrush, or a wild stallion thrashing and bucking while in a confined area. In the past, the fear of disapproval, conflict, or guilt for not following all the rules you're "supposed to" would have pushed these feelings back down, keeping the fire suppressed for another day, another month, another season.

But not now. Not today.

When the breakdown comes, you'll know it. You will feel an overwhelming rejection of all that you've been pretending to be, all of the falseness. Every cell in your body will exclaim, "enough of this!"

Perhaps it's even happening right now. The inevitable breakdown accelerates to its complete fruition right as you read these words. Try saying this out loud, with full power and conviction:

Enough of this.
Enough of this!
I'm done.

I'm done playing these roles, following all these rules.

I'm done being the nice one who always accommodates others.

I'm done hiding and smiling and pretending.

I'm done!

As this intensity arises in you, power starts to build in your body — a growing readiness for action. By now, your "nice police" has probably arrived on the scene, cautioning or threatening you. It might tell you that you'll ruin everything, get fired, lose relationships, and bring about calamity if you start to act in new and different ways. It will be too hard, too destabilizing, and too painful for you and those around you. Besides, your family won't understand, other people will think you're crazy, and… and…

But once the full breakdown has started, it can't be stopped. And trust me, you don't really want to stop it anyway. In order for a new way of being to emerge, the old way must crumble and die. Let it fall apart. Let the new vision for the new you start to emerge from the ashes of the old, false self that was never really you anyway.

Then, try saying this aloud:

I'm ready.

I'm ready to do something radically different.

I'm ready to be real.

To be bold.

To say what I see.

I'm willing to be disliked.

I'm going to say the thing I want to say, ask the thing I want to ask.

Let myself be who I want to be, go where I want to go, do what I want to do.

I'm taking back my life now. I'm going to show up as me.

Real. Raw. Radically honest.

I'm ready. Now. Now!

NOW!

What do you feel as you say this out loud? Has the breakdown already occurred for you? If so, this is merely reinforcement to strengthen you on the path you are already on. If you're not quite ready, then you may feel a growing sense of fear or resistance to claiming the end of the old and the start of something new.

Your mind might be bargaining, saying: *this all sounds much too dramatic and dangerous to boot. No thank you. I'm just going to make a few small changes to make things a bit better, that's all. I don't need any of this radical change stuff.*

Or, perhaps, right now, as you read these words, an unstoppable, unrelenting force is awakened within you. You may be sitting quietly in your car or house, yet your heart rate may be spiking like you're sprinting uphill.

That's because something big is happening, your body feels it, and your soul feels it. It's your spirit coming alive, it's the fire inside burning bright, attacking the oppressive structures that separate you from you. Let those suckers burn.

Now, in the midst of this intensity. It's time to press the eject button. Not tomorrow. Not next week. Now.

CHAPTER 10

EJECT

The breakdown occurs because your old structures that no longer serve you are crumbling. Not all of them, just the ones that are no longer you. By structures, I mean the seemingly solid things you have created in your mind and the world around you. Belief systems, rules, and how you "should be." These are internal structures that give you a sense of order, stability, and safety.

Your job, the role you play at work, your marriage, where you live, how you tend to act each day — these are all external structures that also give you a sense of predictability, control, and safety.

These structures are like an airplane that has flown peacefully for a long, long time. Now that sucker is heading towards a mountain, and you gotta get out. The time to press the eject button is now.

Not later. Not in a few weeks. Not when I end this relationship or change my job or move to a new city or make more money or get married or have a kid or get my degree.

Radically changing the way you show up in life will never get easier. There will never be a time when it isn't uncomfortable.

Now is the time to show up differently.

Now is the time to speak up. To say what needs to be said. To have the conversation you've been avoiding. To be real.

Now is the time for massive action.

Now is the time for a new you to emerge.

Now.

CHAPTER 11

THE TRUTH

When the pain of staying put exceeds your fear of the unknown, you leap. —Lissa Rankin, MD

"Okay! I'm ready," she said with resolve in her voice. Based on her voice tone and facial expression, it was quite obvious she was nervous. But she was also utterly determined. She had that look of relentless fury that only comes when someone has reached their absolute threshold of suffering and is ready to do whatever it takes to break free. The zealous energy of reckless, courageous desperation. I know it well, for it was the exact same mad energy that launched me into a new way of life many years ago.

"So... what should I do?" she asked me, flashing a genuinely puzzled look. As if she had been so focused on gearing up for the battle, that she had no idea who to fight, or how.

"Simple," I replied. I was prepared for this moment, as I'd seen many people at this exact point in the journey, and I knew what would ultimately set her free. "Tell the truth."

~

Where can you tell the truth right now in your life? Where can you be 5% more real, more authentic, more YOU?

Where have you been hiding, holding back, or avoiding speaking up?

These are all possible places for you to begin the transformation process into a bolder, more authentic version of yourself.

I know this might not be the mind-blasting lightning bolt insight you were hoping for. *Wait, to be more authentic and real... I should start being more authentic and real? That's it...?*

Basically, yes!

In theory, it's quite simple. In practice, it's terrifying as all get out.

I remember the day I hit the eject button. I'd been attending a men's group for a period of time, in which I discovered the source of all my relationship problems: I was too nice. So nice that I didn't even know what a boundary was, let alone being able to set or express them.

I didn't know my way out of the cage yet, but I had seen enough to know I had to get out of there. I was pouring fuel on the fire by reading Brad Blanton's book, *Radical Honesty*, in which he advocates for you to tell the truth. How often? Well, to paraphrase Brad, "All the damn time."

I sat at an outdoor bench on the sidewalk next to a Chinese restaurant, waiting for my food to arrive as I read Brad's brutally direct advice: "Stop being a coward. Start telling the truth."

Having just imploded another relationship due to excessive-niceness-induced anxiety, panic, and generally weird behavior, I was already in a breakdown of sorts. I knew my old way of doing things was no longer viable. A new way seemed risky, uncertain to work, and utterly terrifying. But when the circumstances get bad enough, ejecting into the unknown is better than hitting the mountain. So I jammed the button and shot up into the unknown.

The very next day, I went to my job at Portland State University where I was a resident psychologist for students in the health center. I provided individual therapy, ran groups, danced around my supervisor's insecurities to play the deferential underling, wrote boring process notes for insurance purposes, and attended even more boring, very long meetings that I rarely participated in. I also did random side projects that were assigned to me that no one else seemed to want to do, such as providing a breakout room orientation for future potential students exploring the PSU campus.

It was a temporary gig. I had six months left before I completed my final licensure exams so I could set out on my own, thus completing six years of doctoral training. But I needed to accumulate the hours of training for licensure, and I needed to ensure I did not rock the boat in order to smoothly carry out my role until I made it to the other side. Unfortunately, I also needed to be real. So then, this happened:I walked into the PSU counseling center knowing that it would be different to any other day I'd been there. Heck, it would be different than any other day in my life. Why? Because I was going to tell the truth.

Not part of the truth. Not the side of the truth that would appeal to others. Not the truth packaged in a bouquet of niceties to make it more palatable. No. I was going to tell the whole truth as I saw it at the moment. Raw and real. *Here we go.*

While that day was forever memorable as a turning point in my life, the blow-by-blow details have been lost to the annals of time. Either that or I simply blacked out due to anxiety. In any case, my recollection of that day is a series of bright vivid moments of intensity separated by missing scenes.

I sat across from Rory, a university student who had been plagued by feelings of regret over choices he made during his high school years.

"The reason you're feeling that chronic sense of regret is because you aren't fully living right now."

As I said it, I braced myself for push-back, upset, or perhaps a crumpling into sobbing despair. None of which happened. He paused for a good long moment, taking it what I said. And the conversation moved on from there.

As you read that sentence, it may seem like no big deal. Heck, it might be what you'd actually want a counselor to point out to you. But for me, it was very significant. I'd spent my entire life — both socially and professionally — phrasing things as carefully as possible so as to not upset anyone, ever. In this instance, however, I simply said what I saw happening to Rory.

So far, so good.

Later, I was in a meeting with the head of the clinic and a number of the other counselors. Alan was doing what Alan generally did, which was holding the contrarian view to debate something that didn't really need much debating because it wasn't that big of a deal anyway. Instead of being silent and letting Alan eat up meeting time minutes, I spoke up.

"Alan, I noticed that you often take an oppositional stance in these meetings. It doesn't seem like you're particularly interested in hearing other people's perspectives either."

My heart was beating like a jackhammer. This was it. I was doomed. I was a lowly post-doc; Alan had been at this clinic for a decade, and the head of the clinic would surely call me into her office after this meeting and let me know I was fired.

Alan replied in a defensive manner, which was fairly predictable. My goal wasn't to change Alan. My goal was to be real. The meeting continued and we all dispersed afterward. No lingering looks from the clinic director. No dread-inducing, admonishing commands to "Come see me later in my office." Nothing.

It was almost as if me being radically more real wasn't even that big of a deal. In fact, I bet my clients and colleagues didn't even really notice. Or if they did happen to notice a difference, it would be met with mild curiosity. "Huh? Aziz being different? Oh, yeah. I guess so. Whatever."

Next, I met up with my postdoc colleague and a good friend at the clinic, Banjo, for our lunchtime assigned duty. It was a visiting week for potential students of the university, and they had "breakout sessions" available for the students and their parents. One of these breakout sessions was about resources available to students on campus.

One of those resources was the counseling center, of which we were a part. Therefore, our being there to tell students about the counseling center made sense. What didn't make much sense is that our breakout session actually covered all kinds of resources available to students, including the cafeteria, gym facilities, intramural sports and tons of other things that neither I, Banjo, or anyone else at the counseling center had any idea about.

As lowly postdocs, the unpleasant task was kicked down to us. Given that there wasn't really anyone below us on the totem pole, we showed up for the noon breakout. Fortunately, we'd done this several times before, and we were armed with a slideshow presentation that had tons of slides that we basically walked through and read aloud to the audience filled with nodding-off parents in a post-lunch food coma. Death by PowerPoint.

So as to not appear as ignorant fools, Banjo and I read out the bullet points of the slides in an animated and knowledgeable manner, implying that we knew all these factoids about the gym and other resources and so much more.

A student raised his hand partway through the presentation and asked a question about the dormitory situation. I didn't know the answer to that one. A quick glance over to see the bewildered expression on Banjo's face indicated he didn't either. In previous presentations, when I didn't know something, I would either make something up, or give some vague answer that didn't really answer the question or reveal that I didn't know the answer.

Not today.

I told the student that I didn't know the answer to that. I went on to address the crowd of students and parents, who were partially paying attention, partially focusing on their Subway sandwiches and other lunch foods.

"Actually, I work at the counseling center and can tell you quite a bit about that service. All other services I don't really know much about at all. We are just given this slide deck and told to share it with you. No one else from the clinic wanted to do it, so here we are."

The room fell silent, and several parents who'd been zoned out in a meatball sub trance paused to look up, wide-eyed. I stood there, letting the awkward moment of honesty ride for a bit. I was beginning to enjoy this radical honesty thing.

Parents and students stared at me in surprise. Some had startled looks on their faces. Some smiled. Banjo looked mortified at me for having blown our cover.

And then something fascinating happened... The entire energy of the group changed. Students started sharing more. The topic veered towards the counseling center and mental health. People began sharing their fears of leaving for college, or challenges with anxiety and depression, in a room full of strangers they'd never met.

I was surprised and delighted to see that my admission of ignorance, combined with the courage to be radically honest, opened up a new possibility for others in the room. It was a transformative moment where I saw that honesty, even awkward, embarrassing honesty, could actually be powerfully beneficial and healing.

On the walk back to the counseling center, Banjo asked me what the hell was going on. I told him about my plan to be radically honest, and he listened with amusement and horror. He was used to me being a man of extremes by now, but this one felt particularly dangerous to him.

"So... no filters?" he asked.

"No filters." I affirmed. "Well," I added after thinking about it for a minute. "I mean, I'm not going to stand up on my chair in a meeting and pee on the table or anything."

He laughed. I laughed too. I didn't bother telling him that during some of my most bored moments during staff meetings I had actually entertained myself by imagining peeing on the table and visualizing exactly how each staff member would react. There was no point in telling him that. He thought I'm crazy enough as it is.

The day carried on, and there were many moments of honesty, discovery, and discomfort, and there were moments where I still held back. I didn't tell my supervisor that I thought she was highly insecure and constantly needed to establish that she was right and that everyone should follow her rules. That just seemed too dang risky and unclear how it could end well. Especially given that I needed to keep this position long enough to get my hours for licensure. I bet Brad Blanton would've said it.

I finally made it to the end of the day, exhausted, yet fascinated. I felt like I had lived more in that one day than in the last month, or even year.

While I didn't adopt radical honesty as a permanent way of life, this experiment did kick the doors off the cage of niceness and gave me a taste of realness. And I wanted more...

CHAPTER 12

THE TRUTH, PART 2

"**Y**ou are a very self-absorbed person."

I paused to reread this last message. I was just about to get on my bike to ride home when I saw a notification on my phone. My girlfriend had texted me. *Oh, I wonder what she's saying? Maybe something about getting together later that evening, or how awesome I am?*

Nope. I received that delightful gem.

No, we weren't fighting at that moment. She would just randomly tell me things like this with no context or explanation. She apparently had also taken a page out of Brad Blanton's book and was experimenting with telling it like it was. I'm not sure what Brad's love life was like, but for me, this style felt pretty brutal.

So it went with Megan. She wanted to be real and honest, and I did too. Sort of. But in the area of dating, love, and relationships I had followed so many rules for so long that honesty felt painful and confusing.

Should I text her back and tell her that she's a mean, cold-hearted bitch? That's honestly how I felt at that moment. I resisted that urge, though, imagining that's not exactly the "healthy honesty" I was going for.

Man, I'm in over my head here, I thought. *I need more training.*

Which is exactly what I got.

I spent the next three years immersing myself in group environments where I could practice being direct, assertive, and authentic while at the same time doing so with kindness and skill. One of my best teachers on the subject is a woman named Candace, who taught workshops on honesty and authentic connection.

At one of these workshops, I was in a group of three students, including a woman named Rebecca. I noticed that Rebecca talked a lot, but didn't reveal that much in what she was sharing. She seemed emotionally guarded, and I found it hard to connect with her. I felt a sense of aversion and hoped I wouldn't be partnered with her again in the future.

During one of the breaks, I was talking with Candace, and I mentioned I had a challenge with one of my partners. Given my rule of "You should never dislike anything about anyone ever," I imagined Candace would stop me right there and say:

"Wait a minute, Aziz, are you disliking someone? How bad and awful of you. We don't like your kind around here."

Instead, she seemed genuinely curious. "What student? What did you find challenging?"

"Ah..." she said after I had shared. "I've noticed that about her too. She uses language to veil herself rather than reveal herself."

Whoah. Who talks like that?

Candace did (and still does, too), and I wanted to be able to as well.

She had a way of observing others and describing what they were doing with such nonjudgmental clarity.

Flash forward to this day and we've been together for 13 years now. There have been hundreds of times where she has pointed out what I'm doing, even when I'm in an upset or immature state with such kind directness that I have to laugh because it's undeniably true.

Speaking the truth is not simply a decision that you make, such as moving or buying a car. You may start with a moment of decision to be more honest and real, but this is followed up with a process of building your skill and capacity to actually do so. It's much more like deciding to learn to play the guitar or get in shape.

You will learn how to be more skillful at speaking the truth through doing it. This book will give you guidance on how to speak up with both directness and kindness, which you then must turn into a regular practice to see life-changing results.

And, no matter how kind, speaking what is true for you at the moment will inevitably cause pain to others. This last sentence is extremely important, because many people spend their entire lives holding back, playing nice, and living a life that is not their own because they never want to cause pain to others.

While this is certainly a noble desire, it is absolutely incompatible with living an authentic life. Heck, it's probably unachievable even if you tried to be the most pleasing, nice person in the entire world. But it's certainly not going to happen if you have any desire to live a life that is your own.

Humans are destined to feel pain, I'm afraid. There is no one who is exempt from this facet of life. Physical pain, loss, craving, dissatisfaction, sadness, grief, longing, hurt, anger, upset, and on and on. Oh yes, each and every one of us is going to have our fair share of pain in this life.

You cannot stop this. You cannot stop all forms of pain for yourself, for your children, for your parents, for your partner, for friends or colleagues or clients. Pain is inevitable.

While this might not seem like the most inspiring pep-talk, it's the truth, isn't it? In fact, one of the greatest forms of pain is resistance to the pain that manifests as endlessly seeking a way to never experience pain. This leads to a life of avoidance, hiding, holding back, or desperately searching for the next magical practitioner or technique to remove all pain.

So not only is this fool's errand a complete impossibility, attempting to protect others from pain at all costs only ends up causing more pain for you and them.

A recent example of this was with one of my clients, Adam, who'd been dating a woman for about half a year. While he loved and appreciated many things about her, he was clear that being in a long-term committed relationship with her was not the best fit for him.

But how could he tell her this in the right way? Adam had no answer to this question, so he simply stayed in the relationship for the last two months, alternating between wondering how to break the news to her and talking himself out of leaving.

It's a good thing he was coaching with me and brought it up in one of the mastermind calls. I've spoken with clients who had stayed in relationships for these exact same reasons for literally years longer than they wanted to.

To help prepare him for the conversation he didn't want to have, we did several role-plays in the group. He got a chance to hear from me and others and practice what he might say. This not only gave him new skills, it also helped him overcome his fear of this kind of direct contact in which both of them might experience painful emotions.

Ultimately though, no matter how compassionately Adam speaks, she will probably feel upset. She may feel sad, disappointed, hurt, or angry, or unworthy. I mean, how have you felt when someone you were into didn't want to be with you? Probably not fantastic.

But he doesn't have control of that. You don't have control of that. I know I'm being redundant here, but I'm going to say it yet again because we sure tend to operate as if we do have control. So here it is again: you do not have control of how others feel. You don't control how they will interpret what you say, what they will make it mean, or what emotional buttons it pushes in them.

Of course, you can take responsibility for your communication to ensure it is clear, direct, and respectful. That would mean removing character attacks such as "you're an unworthy loser and that's why I'm leaving you."

You can use I language, such as, "This isn't working for me. I want something different." We'll get more into how to speak up with simple boldness and clarity in the next part of this book. In the meantime, the key takeaway is not just what to say, but claiming your readiness to do it. Even though it might be uncomfortable and both you and others are going to have feelings. Dreaded feelings, ahhh!

Despite the role-play and despite intellectual awareness that it's normal for people to have feelings during a breakup,

Adam didn't look quite ready to take action. So I decided to gently prod him a little bit.

"Or… you could wait," I said. "Perhaps another couple months… or a year or two…"

His anxious look turned to a grimace.

"Two more years of making it work… I mean it's not so bad, is it? Besides, you don't want to hurt her feelings. Just be good and stay in it for another few years. If she wants to get married, maybe you'll do that too so as to not disappoint her," I said.

His grimace broke into a grin, and he laughed at this last statement, shaking his head.

"What?" I asked.

"I get it," he said. "It's ridiculous. I'm going to talk with her."

What just happened there? Adam really saw how life-restricting his rules are, and just how intolerably living by them would be over the long run.

Much like Adam, the rules you have that prevent you from speaking the truth and living your life are extreme, life-restricting and often absurd. They appear to be about morality and "goodness" but are entirely focused on seeking safety through stability and preventing short-term discomfort.

But look at where they are leading you. Sure, they might avoid the discomfort of conflict today, but where does that leave you in a month or a year? Usually in the exact same spot… or worse.

Take a moment to follow those rules further into the future to see where they're taking you. If it makes you grimace, good. Let the pain of that suffocating future motivate you to get out there now and start being real now.

CHAPTER 13

THE FEVER

Speaking up for yourself and being more real are probably not new ideas for you. In fact, you've probably thought about this and even tried in the past to be less nice and more real. When I see people attempt this, however, they usually don't last long. Here's why.

First, they are not aware of their rules and how much those are controlling their lives. It feels so wrong to be more direct that they will often stop before they start, writing off the desire to be more authentic as both selfish and unrealistic.

If they manage to push through, and speak up with more directness and truth, they imagine they'll feel empowered, strong, and good. Instead, they feel sick.

This is what I call "the fever."

Now, I don't want to bring about anything unpleasant into your world. It's possible that as you use this book to become a more bold, authentic version of you that you don't experience this fever thing at all. If so, fantastic. But if you do, it goes something like this: after being more real with a colleague and having a direct conversation, or telling your spouse what you really want, you may enter into new territory, you have a conversation that you've never had, one that is unscripted, raw, and real. You both learn something. In the moment it might feel scary, uncertain, wide open, or even exhilarating or deeply connecting.

But by the time you get home, or later that evening, the fever kicks in. Just to be clear, this fever is a metaphor for a storm of emotional discomfort, confusion, and overall pain that you can't quite name. You may feel small, scared, disoriented, confused, hurt, sad, fatigued, or extreme guilt. You may be battered by an intense physical, mental, and emotional storm of shame.

This is so important to know about because, in the absence of support and coaching, many clients tell me that in the past, when they encountered the fever, they took it as a sign that they were doing something wrong and to go back to being pleasing and nice.

But actually, it's the opposite. It's not a sign of you doing something wrong or getting worse. In fact, it's a sign of you getting well.

For many years, I've had the opportunity to participate in many different ceremonies from various religions, cultures, and spiritual traditions. Often, these ceremonies involve the use of plant medicines to facilitate cleansing, healing, and opening of the heart and mind. One common component of taking these medicines can be to heave, vomit, or "purge."

When I first discovered this, like most people, I thought, *I sure hope I don't barf during the ceremony. That sounds terrible.* Only in all these traditions the purging is not seen as a problematic side effect, but rather a central component of the healing. In the Native American church, instead of calling it "getting sick" they call it "getting well."

Over the last fifteen years or so, I've participated in a large number of Santo Daime ceremonies, which involve the use of ayahuasca as you sing Portuguese hymns about the elements, mother earth, and Jesus. Inevitably at some point in the ceremony, I will feel the hot, disoriented feeling arising in which I know purging is coming.

Rather than getting scared, resisting the discomfort, or fighting it in any way, I know that whatever needs to move through me, it's better out than in. I know that as I purge I am releasing stored emotion, old defenses, and pain. This pain is not just my own, but from my family, my lineage, clients, and the broader world. The "sickness" of the purging burns away all that doesn't serve me, and I inevitably leave a ceremony feeling more tender in my heart, more open to intimacy, more capable of loving deeply, and truly be of service in this world.

The same is true for the fever that accompanies speaking up. As you enter into the breakdown phase and begin making a major change in your life, you are penetrating deep layers of defense. These are the walls you put up that block you from others, from yourself, and from life.

Why did you put those walls up in the first place? To defend you from pain.

So what's waiting on the outside of those castle walls? An army of pain!

But instead of being scared of it, or permanently retreating back within the walls to live out a regrettable life that is not your own, the secret path to liberation is to have the courage to face it. Indeed to welcome it as a necessary part of the process that is actually opening your heart, upgrading toxic old beliefs, and reconnecting you with others.

That sick feeling is life getting in. Life healing you. That sick feeling is you finally getting well.

CHAPTER 14

DANCE WITH DISCOMFORT

"Have you ever danced with the devil in
the pale moonlight?" – The Joker

Things are about to get real. We're rounding the corner on the exploratory phase of the book and fast approaching the get off your butt and start doing stuff chapters. They will guide you into healthy conflict, assertiveness, and bold expression so you can become the truest, most authentic version of you now.

This also happens to be the part of the book where those who are going to stop reading will stop reading. Well maybe not this chapter, but they'll make it one or two more chapters into the next section. Then, with all the best intentions, put the book down and say, "Wow, this is great stuff! That Dr. Aziz guy is so smart and handsome. I'll certainly come back to this later and make all those changes. Right now though, I have to go make some guacamole."

It turns out that a bowl of guacamole takes six months to make, and by then, life has moved on. That person is back in the cage of niceness, settling for another period of months or years before the call to more pulls them towards the edge again.

Your life will not change on the edge. Pacing by the side of the pool doesn't get you any closer to jumping in. The change happens when you leap. Not just once, but repeatedly.

So why don't we do it? In a word — discomfort.

Indeed, this path of true liberation is not for the faint of heart. It requires a commitment to courage as you will face challenges from both within and without. Internally, you will confront old rules that have been in place for decades, thereby challenging the beliefs of parents, religion, and the cultural field in which you grew up. This can trigger feelings of anxiety, guilt, shame, or general badness.

You know what life in the cage is like. Yes it's confining, limiting, boring, painful, frustrating, and maybe even life-draining and terrible. But it's familiar, and you're still alive. Part of you might convince you that stepping outside of this cage will lead to death — the death of your relationships, career, ties with family, and everything else in your world. For years this story may have successfully spooked you into retreating away from the exit, back into the corners of your cage.

Outside of this inner discomfort, there's the outer challenge of the actions you will take. Messy conversations, taking the risk to be honest without knowing what that will lead to, and the possibility of — gasp — conflict.

Now, while this all might sound quite daunting, let me share with you some good news. In fact, to break the tension and put a smile on your face, I'll share it in the same manner in which my six year old son approached me the other day.

I was to my elbows in mud cleaning out an irrigation box when he burst out the front door and raced across the yard towards me.

"Dad!" he said, panting to catch his breath.

"Yeah?"

"I have good news and bad news for you. Which do you want first?" he said.

I smiled as I'd never heard him use this phrase before. I also felt a slight sinking feeling in my stomach as I always do when someone says this. My mind jumps to the bad news being utterly catastrophic.

"Hmm," I replied, pondering if I wanted the bad or good first. I always go with bad, personally. I mean how on earth could I enjoy the good news when the bad news might be utterly catastrophic!

"Let's go with the bad news," I said.

"Well…" he paused. "Actually I don't know if it's good or bad," he said, looking confused.

"Oh" I said. We looked at each other in silence as he seemed to try and recall the news.

"Okay," he said, beginning again. "I have two newses for you."

"Okay, great. Tell me the two newses."

If you're not smiling now, perhaps you had to be there. As a side note, every single one of my books has people that love it and people that hate it. The people that hate them often dislike the personal stories I share. I'm sure if they made it this far, they absolutely loved this last one.

In any case, I have two newses for you.

First, while the path from the painful cage of niceness to the joyful liberation of authenticity is not easy or comfortable, it is absolutely possible and absolutely worth it. I have supported and witnessed thousands of people making this fundamental change in the way they approach themselves, others, and life and it is truly inspiring and beautiful.

If you are reading this book and you've made it through all my personal stories to get this far, then you truly have that calling for more. You're called to live a bigger life, a life of courage and honesty and connection. To hold nothing back, give your gifts fully and live the life that is truly right for you, the one you're meant to live.

That call, that hunger, will give you all you need to make it through these first challenges. And the more you practice speaking up and being more real, the stronger you get at it and the more skillful you become, thus making it easier and more natural.

The other piece of newses I have for you is based on directly watching thousands of people go through this process and seeing what works and what doesn't work. Those that succeed wildly differ from those that remain kinda sorta the same in only one key way. It's not their education, age, past experience, the severity of symptoms, gender, wealth, intelligence, or physical appearance. Those that succeed in breaking free all share this one quality: willingness.

More specifically, they are willing to be uncomfortable. They are ready and willing to go into discomfort in order to set themselves free.

Those who try to break free while still remaining comfortable end up not changing that much. They might speak up a little bit here and there. They might even improve some of their life circumstances. But for those that experience a radical shift, enjoying the joy of social freedom to be themselves around anyone, every single one of them has been wildly willing to be uncomfortable.

For them, staying the same is intolerable. And even though they are scared or uncomfortable to try something new, they want the change so bad it's basically a done deal. It's not *if* they are going to take action, it's more of a question of how to work with the discomfort because they know they're going to take action.

Are you at this place now?

Before I coach anyone in my group programs, I ask about their level of motivation to overcome these challenges on a scale of 1 to 10. I'm looking for those who are a 10. Actually, my favorite are those who put eleven. Once in a while, someone will write 100, which always makes me smile.

What level are you? Take a moment now to slow down and really investigate. Don't just give the "right" answer of "ten," as if you're taking a test at school. I invite you to become truly curious. How willing are you to do whatever it takes to be less nice and more boldly authentic, confident, and free?

So, what you got? I'm going to guess if you picked up this book and it made it this far then you're probably above five. Are you a seven? Eight? Nine?

If you're anything less than a ten, why? Why not a ten?

Most people who I ask this question tell me they've tried before and were unsuccessful. They remember these past attempts and question if they have what it takes to really make these changes in a significant way.

Other people tell me that they struggle to stay consistent, that they will take action for a period of time, then tend to fade and drop off after a few weeks or months.

At this moment, I typically point my finger at them and repeat in a deep tone: "Shame. Shame. Shame."

No, I'm kidding. There is no shame here, no good or bad, right or wrong. There's just you and your fear and your heart and your calling and your life. Ultimately, you get to choose how it all unfolds. Do you choose to listen to your heart and heed the call in your soul? Do you choose to risk and open yourself to connections, relationships, and new opportunities and life?

Or do you choose to prioritize safety through the familiar and comfort? Do you shy away from the unknown because it feels too unpleasant, instead focusing on what is easier in the short-term?

That is completely your choice. As the captain of your ship, I can't tell you what is right for you. I know personally I reached a point where imagining another month, let alone another year, or another decade of living the way I'd been living, became utterly intolerable. I felt the pain of years of my life not being fully lived, and it radically exceeded the pain of short-term risk, rejection, and discomfort. And so, I lept.

With sweaty palms and shaky knees, I started trying out new actions that didn't "feel like me" yet. I spoke when my voice quivered and put myself out there when I didn't know what would come back. I bumbled into awkward interactions and had some painfully embarrassing first interactions and rejections. At the time, they were cringy and painful, but honestly not nearly as bad as I had imagined. Plus, even the pain of failing felt better than the numb pain of life on the sidelines.

So I continued — unskilled, trying, failing, and most of all, learning. Which is what exactly will happen for you and what I see in every one of my clients who stays with the process. They learn rapidly. They grow faster than ever before.

If you feel that you are ready for a major change but question if you can pull it off on your own, there's no shame in that. In fact, you might actually be seeing clearly. I call this the "myth of the lone wolf," in which people think they should be able to watch a bunch of YouTube videos and master something as major as changing their entire approach to life. The truth is we need others, and we need to be part of a pack to produce rapid and radical change. I did not make these changes in my life without immersion in training, group programs, and coaching.

If you are curious to learn more about my group coaching programs and if they might be a good fit for you, I invite you to learn more by clicking on the coaching tab of my website https://www.draziz.com.

I encourage you to reflect on the questions I've been asking you in these last few pages. If you truly are ready and willing, then continue on to the next part of this book. If you are less willing, you may want to get curious as to why you are prioritizing comfort over courage, safety over growth.

Sit with it for a few days... where is this choice leading you in your life? What do you imagine will be different in five years? If it's "nothing much," is that okay with you?

Only you can decide, my friend. And when you do decide to leap, to bet on yourself, to claim a new version of you and a new life, then keep reading and your life will never be the same again.

PART III

CONFLICT

CHAPTER 15

THE ROTTEN RULE

"Unknowingly, we seek weakness through safety rather than strength through freedom." — Aleks svetski

Somewhere along the way, most people learned a rule that is not only false, but also has a horrendous impact on their lives. This rule can be summed up as:

*If I, **in any** way, cause someone to get upset or uncomfortable, then I am a bad person.*

This one is a doozy. It might seem like it's a rule born out of the virtue of kindness or caring. I don't want you to feel emotional pain, so I'm going to be thoughtful about what I say or do. But this rule is actually quite different from that mature consideration. It is fueled by fear and has a child-like simplicity to it. Let me explain.

Conflict is when two people see things differently or want things to be done differently. Depending on the issue, how important people feel it is, and how strong their need to get their way, they can experience different levels of upset.

For example, I want to go out to dinner, and you want to stay in. We are having a conflict. Hurray! Now, this is unlikely to be a nuclear conflict, as it is a relatively minor issue. But what if I want to move and you don't. Or do I think you should work less or not spend time with a certain friend that you like? These might lead to greater upset. So you see, often, the more important the issue, the more someone might get upset during this conflict.

Which is what makes the above rule so dang rotten. No one wants to be a "bad person." That triggers the shame response in people and makes them feel terrible, so they avoid it at all costs. Now you're running around trying to avoid people getting upset at all costs.

If you're really nice, you don't just avoid disagreeing on the big stuff. You bend over backward to accommodate others on hundreds of small things throughout your day. Everyone else's preferences take priority over your own, less you cause upset, discomfort, or any negative feelings in others. You don't want to do that, do you? That would make you a bad person.

This one rule is at the root of the majority of your current challenges in relationships and life. It prevents you from honoring yourself and your own preferences, desires, feelings, and dreams. It disconnects you from yourself and sends you down a path of living the life you're supposed to live to please everyone else, but not that life that is your own (the number one regret of the dying, remember?).

Worse still, it will cause you to stay in circumstances and relationships that clearly are not right for you — from romantic relationships to work environments. Have you ever stayed in something longer than you really wanted to because you were afraid of hurting or upsetting the other person (and, therefore, being a "bad person").

I've seen clients tolerate poor treatment, being disrespected, or even overtly teased, mocked or criticized without fighting back, defending themselves, or even speaking up. This, after all, could upset the other person, creating more conflict, which would make my client a bad person.

A rotten rule, indeed.

It's time to change all this once and for all.

CHAPTER 16

REALITY CHECK

Let's take a moment to zoom up and out. Out of your rules and what you learned you should be or shouldn't be like. Let's take a bigger, broader perspective so you can see what's really going on.

Let's start in the beginning, shall we. You, my friend, are a human born on this planet we call Earth. Now, before you roll your eyes and skip ahead, stick with me for a second. All of a sudden, you just popped into this body, awake, conscious as a new being born from your mother. Here you are!

What is this place? How can you perceive so much? How are you conscious? Why is there life here and seemingly nowhere else we can see so far? Why does energy cohere into matter and make all these things that we call mountains and buildings and humans and airplanes?

While you may not have answers to these big questions, I'm asking them so you can see the fundamental nature of the Great Mystery that you, I, and all of us reside within. You may look at all the order of society — the governments, corporate structures, roads and plumbing and supply chain systems and think: *humans got it going on. We sure know what's what.*

Actually, we are just figuring it out as we go, shooting forward at breakneck speed on the tip of the spear of the information age. We don't know where we're going. We don't know what's going to happen in a hundred years, or in a decade. Heck, you and I, we don't really know what's going to happen tomorrow.

All that you see around you is made up by other humans. Not just the cars and buildings and cell phones, but also all the ideas and philosophies, and rules. Many of the rules you live by, you simply got from your parents, who got them from their parents, who got them from their parents, who... well, you get the idea.

While you may want to honor and appreciate your mother and father, and whoever raised you for loving, supporting, and contributing to you during your life, I would caution you from imbuing their reality with some sort of ultimate authority. The truth is they are just another being like you and me and all those you see around you. They just happened to be born twenty or thirty or forty years before you. They just popped through the portal first.

I've met clients who have been living in their dad's or mom's reality their entire lives. They're in their sixties, their dad has been dead for many years, and they're still living out the toxic, limiting rules and stories laid forth for them. Can you relate?

Why are you doing it? Why are you continuing to give your authority and power away to someone else, especially in ways that don't really serve you? Of course, your mind might immediately say, *I can't help it. These rules just feel true, and I can't break them.*

But you and I both know that's B.S. Those very same clients who live under the toxic thumb of these old rules often treat their children very differently. They want their kids to be freer, so they encourage free thinking, expression and authenticity in them. In essence, they defy the old rules for their children but not for themselves. So the truth is it's not about capability. It's about deserving. And on some level, they don't think they deserve a better life.

Now, why would they, or you, think you don't deserve better? Because you're confused, misguided, or disoriented from the truth, disconnected from the Great Mystery. Whatever makes you feel unworthy or less than others is certainly made up by humans and involves rules as well. Rules that you got from your parents, who got them from their parents, who...

In sum, humans are running around making things up. It's presented to you from an early age that it's part of a grand plan of order and control, and that it all makes sense. You assume the rules of your family and the society around you all are there for a reason and must be followed.

Your liberation comes when you see through this. When you start to become the captain of your own ship, choosing not only which rules to follow but also the values by which you will navigate this life.

What if we frankly said to children, "How do you do? Welcome to the human race! We are playing a game and we are playing by the following rules: we want to tell you what the rules are so that you know your way around, and when you understand what rules we are playing by, when you get older, you may be able to invent better ones."

— Alan Watts

CHAPTER 17

WHAT BOUNDARIES REALLY ARE

As you transform your relationship with conflict and disagreement, you will feel an incredible sense of liberation in your daily life. You'll no longer be carrying that cage of niceness and fear around with you everywhere you go and instead, you'll feel a spacious sense of possibility in all your relationships and in your life.

This chapter and the ones that follow will help you see conflict, and indeed yourself, in a new light so that you are able to speak up in bold and courageous ways like never before. If you find this process overwhelming, know that you're not alone.

I work with clients in these exact situations every day, and should you want additional support, I encourage you to reach out at www.lessnicebook.com/coaching. I've found profound changes often occur in a pack rather than when we try to lone wolf it.

Let's start with what boundaries really are. Contrary to the immature perspective of the rotten rule, differing perspectives, desires, and opinions are inevitable, healthy, and necessary in all your relationships. In other words, it's impossible for you to always think and feel exactly the same as others and to desire the same things at the same time.

Should you get hungry at the same time as your friend, always wanting to eat exactly what they eat? It sounds absurd when you look at it that way, and yet this is what you might be pressuring yourself to do all the time.

This pressure to align yourself completely with others comes from an underlying belief that differences are bad and dangerous. *If I am not exactly like you, a photocopy of your thoughts, feelings, and desires, then you won't like me, or you'll leave me.*

You most likely concluded this at a young age when a parent or other authority figure yelled at you, criticized you, or otherwise labeled you as "bad" for overstepping one of their boundaries or rules.

This judgment may have been intense or mild, occasional or daily. It may even have come from the best intentions of your parents, or sometimes slipped out in their weaker moments of stress or irritability.

If you are a parent, you know that, like a pitcher, you have your "on" days and your "off" days. Sometimes you are throwing strong, dealing with messes, resistance, and the irrational chaos of your kids with patience, flexibility, and general awesomeness. And then, some days... not so much.

A while ago, I walked upstairs to see my five-year-old son, Arman, drawing on the wall with a pen. My initial reaction was exasperated irritability, no doubt the result of some victim story along the lines of: *I do so much around here, and you're making even more work for me.*

My impulse was to make a big show of how that's "against the rules" and "we don't draw on the walls" and throw around timeouts left and right. That, my friends, is justice! Yet, for some reason, I didn't do all of this and paused instead... perhaps due to the brightness and enthusiasm on his face.

I told him we couldn't draw on the walls with a pen but that we could draw on paper downstairs. I took the pen and walked downstairs with him, where he moved on to some other game. I did express a boundary but didn't make a big deal of it either.

Later that evening, Arman was lying in bed with his mom, reading a book. He interrupted her to tell her about the picture he'd been drawing on the wall. He told her all about who was in the picture and what they were doing. He led her from the downstairs bedroom upstairs to his room, telling her, "Here's me. I'm holding hands with daddy and closest to him because I love him the most. Here's you, Zaim, and part of grandma. I was going to finish drawing her and grandpa, but Dad took my pen away."

When I heard about this, my heart broke. This wasn't an act of defiant vandalism to stick it to his parents. This was a little boy creatively expressing how much he loved his family.

Whew! I was so glad I didn't go ballistic when I caught him drawing on the walls. I think the reason I held back is that I felt the love and enthusiasm emanating from him, and the last thing I wanted to do was communicate the message: *If you cross one of my boundaries, you are a bad human.*

Yet at the same time, I didn't ask him any questions about his drawing. I didn't get curious and really explore what was going on.

So what does this have to do with boundaries, being less nice, and being more you? It turns out, everything. Because boundaries are nothing more than our preferences. They're not facts, or commands, or demands, or how things "should be" in the world. It might seem like that, but there's always so much more going on than meets the eye.

So instead of totally conforming to what you imagine everyone else wants, or firmly declaring your boundaries with entitled demand, what if you simply shared your preferences? What if someone else was doing the same with you, when they were saying what they wanted or didn't want?

It doesn't mean you're bad, or that you have to feel crinkled up and ashamed. Even if someone communicates their boundaries in a blaming, unpleasantly demanding way. You don't have to take that on. You can let that flow by like sludge in a river. You don't have to reach your hand in, scoop it up, sniff it, and put it in your boat. For God's sake, just let that black goo float on by!

So the next time someone is going on and on about "you said this and didn't do that, and you never do this, and…" you can listen and get really curious. I wonder what it is they prefer. I wonder what expectation they had that has been broken?

You can even ask them. "So you would prefer to have more time for yourself in the mornings? I want to hear more and understand what matters to you."

If you automatically react to someone else being upset with chills of terror or a clenched stomach, then you might not know the difference between expectations and agreements and what your responsibilities really are. In fact, you're probably taking way too much responsibility for, well, everything.

CHAPTER 18

EXPECTATIONS VS. AGREEMENTS

I learned this distinction from Steve Chandler, and it's been profoundly helpful in my life, not just for communication purposes but to relieve my chronic nice-person stress from taking on way too much responsibility for everything around me.

Expectations are your unspoken desires of how you want things to go. As humans, we generally have expectations about, well, everything. You have expectations for yourself, your family, friends, pets, coworkers, boss, clients and customers, public figures, politicians, and strangers. You even have expectations for life around you — the weather, traffic, geopolitics, and the economy.

This is completely natural, and expectations in themselves aren't bad. The mind is an evaluating machine, constantly putting all of life into categories and boxes to get control, predict the future, and avoid pain. The most common category the mind puts everything into is either the "good" box or the "bad" box. It's constantly doing this.

If you'd like to see this for yourself, take a few minutes and just observe your mind at any moment throughout the day. Every thought, feeling, person, event, object, and circumstance has a valence to it. A sense of attraction or aversion, like or dislike, good or bad. It's like a whirring fan, that mind, with all its incessant evaluations.

This isn't necessarily a problem, and it's just what the mind does. The problem is when you attempt to meet everyone else's expectations. Are you trying to do this? Hustle to meet everyone's unspoken expectations about how you should be and what you should do?

What if I expect you to dote on my every word, listen to my 45-minute instructions about how I like my toast prepared, and only refer to me as "Budda-Jesus" or "Your Eminence" without looking me directly in the eye?

But seriously, what if I have unreasonable expectations? What if I expect you to always respond to me within one hour, no matter what's going on in your life? What if I expect you to drop everything and pay attention to me, even without me asking for it? What if I expect you to never tell me "no" or that means you don't love me?

Other people's expectations don't even have to be unreasonable, and they might just not work for you. I have lots of people who expect me to respond to their emails, social media comments, or otherwise. I don't want to spend all my time at work responding directly to every communication, so that expectation doesn't work for me.

I've had people expect that I should give away all my coaching services, including my 12-month mastermind program, for free. They said that if I really cared about helping people, this is what I would do. I pointed out that I have hundreds of hours of free teachings on YouTube videos and in podcasts, but these people have an expectation for more.

That also doesn't work for me.

Which, by the way, is a great question to start asking yourself. Instead of "what do they want of me?" with a pressured feeling of needing to meet whatever the expectation might be, you can ask yourself, "does that work for me?"

If it doesn't, what would work for you? How do *you* want it to go? This helps you uncover what your own unspoken expectations are. Once you've discovered them, what should you do?

Clearly, the answer is to assert dominance and shout your expectation louder, starting with "oh yeah! Well *you* should..."

No, I'm kidding. What you could do is turn your expectations into agreements.

This involves you sharing what you'd like and the other person or people sharing what they'd like and together coming up with an agreement that works for you both. Instead of two people pleasers giving whatever they think they should so the other person isn't upset, you have two real humans putting their cards on the table and creating a powerful agreement that serves them both.

In order for it to be an agreement, it is removed from the private realm of your head and actually spoken out loud, discussed, and has both people on board. The conversation itself doesn't have to involve some formal tone, shaking hands, and signing an agreement contract. It's simply getting clarity on a way of being together that works great for both people.

Here are a few quick examples from clients I've worked with recently on this topic.

Maggie recently had a painful experience in dating in which she thought she was exclusive with a dating partner, but he had also been dating other women. She had the expectation that if they slept together, he obviously wouldn't sleep with anyone else. When she found out he was simultaneously dating other women, she was sad, hurt, and angry. As they'd started dating, Maggie did not have any conversations with him about exclusivity, and they hadn't created any clear agreements.

In her next dating experience, she brought up the conversation sooner, as she was noticing more chemistry and desire. The essence of her communication was: *here is what I'm looking for. What do you want?* This led to clear agreements and a foundation for an extraordinary connection to blossom.

Alex had several team members who repeatedly turned their work in late, which placed undue stress on him. He had the expectation that everyone meets their deadlines, or if they cannot, then they communicate about this and come up with a solution.

As you read this, you might exclaim — *that's an obvious one! Of course, people should get their work in on time. He shouldn't have to create an agreement about that!* You could take that stance and assume it's obvious, get upset and then demand others do it or else. However, this rarely works. And by rarely, I mean never.

This is the perennial story of failed romantic relationships. One or both partners have tons of expectations for the other person and then don't bring them up or talk about them, defensively asserting that "I shouldn't have to ask for that because it's obvious" or the classic "if they really loved me, they would have noticed and done something about it without me bringing it up."

Instead, to have more harmony, connection and ease at work and in all your relationships, you must make a practice of speaking up regularly to turn expectations into agreements. Not only does this actually make things flow more smoothly, you also have more of an influence on what happens in your ongoing interactions and relationships.

Alex told his team members what he expected regarding work submissions and deadlines. He invited team members to share their challenges with meeting these deadlines and their ideas of how to communicate if these deadlines could not be met.

During the conversation, he learned several things he did not know about the processes in his business and discovered some problems that were occurring upstream that lead to these deadline delays. It wasn't just laziness and poor work ethic, which is what he'd been concluding about certain team members.

I wonder, what agreements could you make today?

CHAPTER 19

HURT VS. HARM

While we're on the subject of taking too much responsibility for everyone else's experience, here is a key distinction that can change everything for you.

As a nice person, you most likely value kindness, love, and treating others with respect and care. What are you, some kind of hippie? You've got to crush your enemies and feed on their remains if you want to make it in this world, man. Trust no one.

The problem with over-responsibility is you no longer actually follow your values of kindness and treating others with respect. You veer way off that path and end up trying to care-take everyone, so they don't ever feel discomfort or pain. This isn't kindness, it's insanity.

If there's one thing that humans are guaranteed to experience in this life, it's pain and discomfort. This can range from mild daily discomforts, such as hunger, boredom, or small disappointments, to larger pains, such as major loss, illness, or hardship. You'd be hard-pressed to find anyone, ever, throughout human history who made it through even one day without some discomfort.

Yet I see people all the time avoiding speaking up, being real, or sharing because "I don't want to hurt their feelings." Of course, this goes back to the old classic parental admonition — if you don't have anything nice to say, then stuff it down and sustain unhealthy relationships at the expense of your soul.

Here's the truth about hurt and harm. Hurt is another word for discomfort or pain, which is inevitable, right? People can feel hurt for any reason, regardless if that was your intent or not. Someone might look at you, hoping you'll smile and tell them they're amazing. If you don't, they feel disappointed and hurt. Someone might want you to do their dirty dishes every day, and if you don't, they feel hurt.

The point is people have millions of expectations, and desires and when those aren't met, which they often aren't, they feel some form of discomfort or hurt. You are not responsible for this.

But wait a minute Aziz, aren't I responsible for what I say? What if I say something and it hurts someone's feelings?

Ahh, now we get into the concept of harm. Harm is when you say or do something with the primary goal of causing pain in another. No, that doesn't make you a sociopathic sicko, that makes you human. We all get hurt or angry and then act less skillfully than we want to. Perhaps you are sharp with your words or tone or say something you don't really mean. Or worse, maybe you blow up, spew rage, or even hit someone.

Generally, character attacks, which are blaming statements that essentially tell someone they're globally bad or unlovable, are harmful. *You are an idiot, you are lazy,* etc.

Here's a little rule of thumb to act by if you're unsure. If someone is hurt by something you said or did, ask yourself, *did I communicate what was true for me? Did I do so with respect?*

If so, then it's on the other person to manage their own emotions.

If, on the other hand, you communicated harshly, using blaming words or a shaming tone, or something less respectful than you want to be, then you may have veered into harm territory.

In this case, you may want to reach out, apologize, take ownership and reconnect with the other person. They may forgive you instantly, and all is well, or they may be upset and hold onto that. Regardless, once you've cleaned up your side of things, there's nothing really more to do. Anything lingering is their business, and they will resolve it in their own way, in their own time.

CHAPTER 20

BRAVE

The last few chapters have been clearing the way for you to have more permission to speak up for yourself. Having a boundary doesn't mean you're bad — it just shows you have a preference. Speaking the truth and someone having feelings doesn't make you an awful person — temporary hurt feelings are an inevitable part of this human existence.

As the mist clears and you are able to see the path ahead, it's time to take those next few steps. Steps into the unknown where you don't exactly know what will happen when you do speak up with more honesty, directness, and power. How will that person react? Will it "go well?" Will they like you or dislike you as a result?

As much as you can, I invite you to step outside of this outcome-based evaluation style. Instead of checking after each interaction to see if it was "good" or not, based on how comfortable you or others felt, I invite you to commit to a new way of being. This new way of being involves an attitude that goes something like this:

I am going to speak up and be more real, or at least, as much as I can in all areas of my life. I want to do this because it feels healthy and will ultimately lead to a life that feels fully my own and fully lived.

You can try reading those last few sentences out loud to see how that feels. You can also change the wording to fit your own attitude to this new way of being. Can you feel how it's very different from, "will they like me?" or "am I good enough / pleasing to them?"

Let's assume you are on board with this new attitude and new way of being, and ready to put it into practice. At this point, you have two choices, two ways to approach this new way of life.

Your first option is to do so timidly. I mean you are doing something radically different, unverified, and potentially dangerous afterall. Tread lightly. Don't rock the boat and don't make a mess.

This is a very common way that people step into the unknown in their lives. There is a fantastic video that I like to share at my events and workshops called the Ten-Meter Tower. In it, the filmmakers set up cameras and microphones to capture the reactions people had at the top of a thirty-foot drop into a swimming pool down below. The close-up audio and video footage gives you an intimate look at what people are like as they encounter an action that fills them with fear.

I share this video at my events to help participants witness the wide range of reactions people have to a scary challenge and invite them to observe which approaches seem better or more effective and which ones seem less effective.

Everyone unanimously agrees that slowly pacing to the edge of the diving board, pausing long and hard in a tight, contracted posture while holding your breath, and then pacing back and forth saying a mantra like "I can't do this" is a suboptimal strategy for facing our fear.

And yet this is exactly what we do in our daily lives when it comes to facing that scary challenge coming up on our calendar. We fret and worry and contract our bodies and breathe shallowly while focusing on how we can't do it or we're somehow "not enough." We writhe around in painful "what if" scenarios about all that could go wrong and how we couldn't handle it.

Interesting side note — several people in the ten-meter tower video make some reference to dying from the jump. Their "what if" scenarios include the possibility of death as a result of this leap.

How absurd the audience chuckles to themselves, watching the video from the safety of their own cozy couch. But when you imagine speaking up more freely, saying no to someone, asking for what you want, or simply deciding to be more real without even specifically knowing what you'll say later today… is there some way in which you wonder if you'll die from such a change?

It may be irrational, but it certainly doesn't stop us from fearing it.

So there you have the timid approach. Timid is the mind convincing us that we are much weaker than we really are. Timid is one foot in and one foot out, trying to take the risk without really taking the risk. Timid is destined to fail.

So let's turn our attention to option two: **brave**. In this option you choose to be brave. Is that really a choice we can make? What if I feel tremendous fear? The good news is, you can still choose to be brave. In fact, choosing brave requires that fear be present.

The definition of brave is: *ready to face and endure danger or pain; showing courage.* It's not saying, "Okay, I'll give it a shot and I sure hope it goes easily and smoothly with no discomfort." That attitude lacks courage, and therefore lacks the staying power needed to make these changes actually stick in your life.

You must be willing to lean into that discomfort and hit the waves head-on. And when you do, something magical happens. You'll discover that how you approach discomfort changes your experience of that discomfort.

Let's take the example of someone getting into a cold pool or lake or ocean. There's that person who's "warming up to it" by inching their way in. Half an hour later they've made it up to their thighs and they're thinking about making the leap to getting their crotch in the water. But oh my, it's so very cold!

And then there's the person who cannon-balls into the pool, yelling at the top of their lungs as they do so. Or that crazy fool who runs into the waves, icy water splashing all over their chest, then diving face-first into the water.

In both instances, the water temperature is the same. It's the same kind of cold, same inherent discomfort in the water. But, ask anyone who's tried both approaches and they will tell you that there is a world of difference in how that water feels when you approach it with wild bravery.

So how are you going to approach the opportunities that this day, this week, this season of your life have to bring you? If you know you're going to jump off that tower, or get into that cold water, then do yourself a favor. Acknowledge that little part in there, let's call him Timid Ted or Timid Theressa, and bath him in love and warmth. I get it, it's scary, and I love you, little buddy.

Then stand up, tall and proud. Take a full breath into your body, charging up your vitality, strength, and life force. And in this moment, right now, choose Brave.

And then leap.

Nothing's gonna hurt you the way that words do
When they settle beneath your skin
Kept on the inside and no sunlight
Sometimes a shadow wins
But I wonder what would happen if you

Say what you wanna say
And let the words fall out
Honestly I wanna see you be brave

— *Brave* by Sara Bareilles

CHAPTER 21

THE PENDULUM

One major concern of recovering nice people is that once they step off the restrained shores of passive submission, they will awaken their inner dragon and end up burning all their relationships to the ground. They fear awakening their anger, worried that it will overtake them and cause unnecessary pain and wreckage in its wake.

One way to think of this is like a pendulum, which is an object that is tied to a string and hangs down. When you pull the pendulum to one side and release it, it swings far to the other side, then back towards the starting point, then back to the other side, and so on until it eventually finds its way to rest in the middle.

It turns out there is some truth to this pattern of finding your self-expression that seems to occur for many people. After years of being overly passive, overly accommodating, and overly self-sacrificing, people discover there may be a pool of repressed resentment waiting there underneath that passive persona.

When they do start to speak up, it might have an edge to it. They might be pissed off and tired of being walked all over. Which ultimately is a good thing!

It might seem particularly scary, especially if you've had strong ideas about being nice and not ever hurting other peoples' feelings, but overall it's a necessary stage in the process and something you can give plenty of space for. I often encourage clients to allow themselves to be messy for a little while. It won't last forever.

Besides, the only way to learn how to be totally skillful in communication is through a great deal of practice. Maybe sometimes your tone will be a little sharper or more blaming than you'd like it to be. And other times, you spoke up more timidly and submissively than you'd prefer. That's all okay! Let your pendulum swing around from passive to aggressive as you find your way to assertive in the middle.

To help you orient yourself during this season of discovery, in which you'll find your way to a strong, assertive, clear style of communication, I want to provide you with a little map. You see, many books on assertiveness break communication down into three categories: passive, assertive, and aggressive. In essence, they teach that passive behavior and aggressive behavior are bad. Assertive, right there in the middle, is the tops. So do that.

But after working with clients on this process for years, I realized that more nuance is needed to help you find that middle way of assertiveness.

This map gives you more gradation within the categories of passive, assertive, and aggressive, as well as descriptions of your mindset from each place. This can help you more quickly pinpoint where you are on the spectrum, thus accelerating your learning and ability to communicate skillfully.

STYLE	PASSIVE			ASSERTIVE			AGGRESSIVE		
LEVEL	1	2	3	4	5	6	7	8	9
PATTERN	Say nothing, do everything	Hint at what you want	Say it, then retract it	Say it hesitantly	Say it, direct and kind	Hold your ground	Shut up and listen! It's my time now.	Say it and take it	Intent to injure
OUTCOMES	Frustration, failed relationships, repressed anger & resentment, physical pain, anxiety, depression, being overlooked, not chosen, ignored.			Increased connection, mutual benefit, being listened to, respected, valued, healthy relationships, physical and mental well-being, contribution-focused.			Short term "winning" or domination, success without fulfillment, distanced relationships, retaliation, abandonment, failed relationships, legal or social repercussions		
SELFISH	Self-Denying			Healthy Self-Interest			Other-Denying		
NEEDS	"I have no needs."			"My needs matter and so do yours."			"I care about my needs, not yours."		
MATURITY	Immature			Mature			Immature		
PRIORITY	Safety			Connection / Collaboration			Significance / Being Right		

CHAPTER 22

THE PASSIVE STYLE

Let's start with the Passive Style. In this category, you'll see there are three levels (1-3). The lower the level, the more passive you are. Each level has a pattern that you are running that summarizes your mindset and, therefore, your style of relating to others.

Level 1 is described as "say nothing, do everything." This means you're apt to do whatever others want, even if they don't explicitly ask you. You habitually, maybe even compulsively, give to others without a thought for yourself. The "say nothing" part of this pattern means you don't speak up for your needs, don't ask for what you want and don't disagree or show displeasure with others.

If this sounds saintly or virtuous to you, then you're not alone. Many cultural traditions encourage this selfless way of being, often for one particular group or gender (such as women should be this way). While there may be a time for noble sacrifice in which you completely put yourself aside to serve the needs of the moment, this is generally best used as a conscious, temporary choice in response to a crisis period such as the grave illness of a family member or other extreme times.

If this is expected to be a sustained "normal" way of being, the self-denying nature of it leads to physical breakdown, emotional ailments such as anxiety and depression, and even failed relationships (either in the form of the person ultimately being left despite all their sacrifice, or enduring dysfunctional or even abusive dynamics. Yikes.)

If you spend a lot of time at level 1, it's a good thing you're reading this book. Let's work you up this scale and watch how much better your life can become!

In level 2, we're smack dab in the middle of passive-land. This level is described as "hint at what you want." You are generally still completely oriented towards others and what they want and need, but you do have some inklings of your own thoughts, feelings, and desires. You may even let yourself wish or dream in the privacy of your own mind.

But when it comes to directly sharing those desires or asking boldly for what you want, these are unfortunately not available within this way of being. Instead, you must hint at what you want, by placing little breadcrumbs, passive comments, or even more subtle clues for those around you. Sometimes, it works! Your partner, friend, or family member might pick up on your subtle hint and ask if you'd like something, or even simply fulfill your unspoken request.

More often, however, it doesn't work. These hints are often missed in the hustle and bustle and fullness of daily life. You tell yourself that it's too much to ask for the things you need, that the needs of the family or the workplace or your friends or whoever are too great (aka more pressing than your own).

You also have a slightly distorted view that your hints are very clear and seen by all. And that if the other people really wanted to do the things you hinted towards, they would do them. So if they don't do them, it means they don't want to, which means you can't press on further, for that would be rude, demanding, or open the door to conflict.

You imagine that asking others directly will lead to them either saying "no" and being upset with you for being so needy or demanding, or they will say "yes" out of guilt and burden and fulfill your request with resentment, all of which is very unpleasant.

Furthermore, you live in a world where asking directly for what you want is still somehow deemed as selfish, bad, wrong, or otherwise unacceptable, hence all this dancing around with hints. Good times, this **level 2** stuff.

Let's work our way up to **level 3**, which is at the upper band of the passive world. This level can be summarized as " say it, then retract it." Here, you might be challenging the old conditioning that has forbidden you from asking for what you want or speaking up for yourself. You start to dip your toe in the water of being more assertive; however, the old rules still seem like the right rules, or the "right" way for you to be.

So, if you do float an idea out there, or ask for something more directly, if you catch even the slightest whiff of hesitation or push-back from another person, you hastily and apologetically retract your request.

"I'd love to go to the lake this weekend. It's going to be so nice out." You say in an uncharacteristically direct way, one day in the kitchen.

Your partner, who's standing there with the fridge door open, pondering his next move, doesn't immediately say anything in response. Did he hear you? Is he considering the lake? Is he absorbed in the choice between salad or a sandwich? Who knows! But it's time to abort!

"But we don't have to..." you add to your initial statement.

This dance is quite common at the upper limit of the passive style. Sometimes you will let your desire float a little longer until it's actively questioned or challenged, and then you reign it back in, making it very clear that you aren't demanding anything, that others don't have to fulfill your request, and that it's "no big deal."

These three levels make up the passive style of relating to yourself and others. In the realm of selfishness, this could be called "self-denying," in which your needs and desires are deemed less important than others, typically always. You may not even be fully aware of what you want or need from years of dismissing and downplaying those needs, often questioning if you even have desires or needs in the first place.

This passive style of relating is a lower level of maturity in which you are not skillfully relating to others, creating an adult-adult relationship in which both people are responsible for expressing their desires and needs. Instead, there's more of a child-like quality of wanting to please others and not upset the "adults" — even though you may chronologically be an adult yourself, or even older than the other people you're relating to!

This immaturity is also reflected in certain styles of thinking, such as imagining others should mind-read your desires and needs and magically fulfill them without you having to ask. Or simplistic stories such as "If he really loved me he'd naturally want to do the thing I want him to do, so I shouldn't have to ask him."

Your priority in the passive style of relating is for safety, as opposed to authenticity or growth. You are primarily concerned with preserving the relationships in your life by pleasing others so they won't have reason to leave you. Those relationships and the love you receive within them for being "good" allows you to be safe and survive.

The passive style of relating tends to have certain outcomes or consequences. These include repressed anger and resentment, physical pain and other ailments, anxiety, depression, and being overlooked, not chosen, taken for granted, or ignored. As many of your needs go unmet, you might feel discouraged, depleted, or frustrated.

Despite this being a strategy to preserve relationships, a passive style can actually lead to relationship problems or even failed relationships. The unspoken resentment, lack of real intimacy, and physical and emotional problems that arise out of this way of being can cause strain or distance within relationships, making them more prone to rupture, loss of passion, or dissolution.

But other than that, being passive is great!

CHAPTER 23

THE ASSERTIVE STYLE

As you move up to **level 4** on the map above, you enter into the land of assertiveness. Much like the passive style, the assertive style is not simply one way of being. It actually has its own range in which you can be less or more assertive.

Level 4 is on the lower end of this range in which you do say what you want or ask for something, but with hesitation. This may show up in a halting voice tone, difficulty making eye contact during a statement or request, or otherwise showing an apologetic tone. You may feel the need to offer reasons or explanations for your assertion, still adhering to some of the passive conditioning in which your needs or desires for their own sake are still somehow unworthy or don't warrant sharing without a good deal of justification.

And yet, here you are, speaking up! The nice conditioning may still be whispering dismissing statements to you, but you are undeterred and willing to challenge that. And so you speak up, even if you're nervous. You assert yourself, even if you end up using more words than you want or over-explaining yourself.

And guess what? It still works!

Even when you're not perfect at it, even if it could be done more firmly or directly or boldly. Despite all that, when you speak up for yourself, you end up getting what you want more. Others begin to listen to you and pay more attention. You begin to put your needs into the equation in your relationships, which makes your needs matter to others as well. Now you're ready for the next level.

Level 5 is the sweet spot. This is where you can "say it, direct and kind." What is the "it," you might ask? Whatever it is that needs to be said! Perhaps it's something that's bothering you, or a request that you have. In fact, at this level of assertiveness, you value your own thoughts, feelings, desires, and needs. They become a meaningful component of the information you use to guide your decisions, behaviors, and communications with others.

The "it" that needs to be said might be feedback for someone that you work with or live with. If your role at work requires you to tell others something they are doing wrong and how to do it better, then you do that with directness and respect.

If you see your partner being sharp with one of your kids, you point that out and ask how they feel because they seem irritated. You don't have to load it with judgment or criticism; on the contrary, you might be curious about your partner and what they're hurting or stressed about. But instead of being passive and pretending nothing is happening and not calling it out so as to not upset them, you simply say what is so, as you see it at that moment.

In fact, this is a great summary of **level 5**: *I simply say what is so, as I see it at this moment.*

What happens when you read that sentence out loud several times? Can you feel the ease and spacious permission of being that way? Can you imagine how relieving it would be to bring more of that into your relationships and daily life?

At the next level of assertiveness, **level 6**, you're reaching the upper bounds of this style of relating. At this level, you are able to ask for something or share your perspective and then hold your ground.

This is in stark contrast to the upper bound of the passive realm, Level 3, in which you hastily retract any statement or request that might disagree with the desire or opinion of another. Instead, at this level of assertiveness, you are able to withstand the tension that arises when there are differing perspectives, desires, needs or even views of reality.

Holding your ground doesn't mean pounding the table and attempting to drown out all dissent from your viewpoint. On the contrary, it actually involves being curious about the views of others, knowing that your desires and viewpoints matter, as do those of others. You're able to go into the murky waters of the spaces in between. Places where you might be wrong or not see the situation totally accurately. Places where others might be wrong or distorted in their viewpoints.

From this confusing place of the gray in between, you discover new information, make new decisions, and reach a more intelligent, nuanced level of clarity. You are able to hear differing perspectives and challenge them, ultimately choosing to disagree or not adopt them. You are also able to consciously upgrade how you might see a situation or admit ways in which your perspective is limited.

This level of assertiveness leads to rich, meaningful conversations, problem-solving, and intimacy. It forges deep bonds in marriages and with family. It resolves workplace problems and helps you be a powerful leader who can solve complex problems.

It requires healthy boundaries, cognitive flexibility, humbleness, and compassion for yourself and others. It also requires a more mature view of conflict, differing opinions, and communication overall.

You are no longer bound by the immature beliefs that conflict, disagreement, or upsetting others are inherently bad. You have a more sophisticated understanding of relationships, knowing that all close connections, both personal and professional, will at times involve disagreement, conflict, and finding your way to collaborative solutions.

In fact, this is the priority in this assertive style of relating: connection and collaboration. Instead of just wanting people to like you or never be upset with you so you can stay safe, you are more focused on how you can truly connect with others. You know that real connection requires intimacy which means others see and know the real you and vice versa. That requires the risk of sharing more directly, openly, and honestly.

From this connection, you can truly collaborate with others, whether that's to raise children with a partner, grow a company with team members, or bring a new creative project into the world with the help of others.

This style of relating to others tends to bring about numerous positive benefits. First things first, you get much more of what you want in life when you skillfully and persistently ask for it! You also enjoy better friendships, win-win relationships, and deep, meaningful connections. You feel fulfilled because others listen to you, respect you, and value you. Your physical health is improved because you can prioritize taking care of yourself, and your mental well-being is enhanced because you can speak up at the moment to address your upset rather than chewing on resentment stew all night long.

Being skillfully assertive is not most people's default communication training from their upbringing. Like learning a new language, it takes regular practice to be able to speak, think, and act in this way.

CHAPTER 24

THE AGGRESSIVE STYLE

Alright, now it's time to tell you the truth. While most therapists and so-called "experts" will tell you that assertiveness is the optimal way to relate to others, let me tell you the real truth that "they" don't want you to know.

If you want to get ahead in this world, you gotta be ruthless. Trust no one. Keep your friends close and your enemies closer. When the moment is right, don't hesitate to cut the throats of those around you, for in the end, there can be only one.

No, I'm just messing with you.

The aggressive style, much like the passive style, has a number of problems that arise when it's used as a regular approach to communicating with others. What most people don't realize is that aggressive style communication isn't just reserved for raging narcissistic or overly domineering people. In fact, nice people end up using the aggressive style without knowing it, especially if they've been suppressing themselves into passive-land for way, way too long.

It's important to see when you are using this style so you can steer more towards assertiveness, and when others are using it so you can effectively protect yourself with skillful boundaries.

Level 7, at the lower end of the aggressive style, is when people take the assertive style a bit too far. Perhaps you've been holding back for too long and something inside of you snaps and you can't take it anymore. You're hurt, resentful, and angry and you're no longer going to stuff it down and play nice. The essence of this level can be summarized as "shut up listen! It's my time now."

You feel justified in talking over others, because others have talked over you for too long damnit! There's a righteousness and entitlement to this level, where you demand others listen and you think they should or must do so. Your priority at this level is to reclaim a sense of lost power and significance, not necessarily to truly connect with others.

This level, and all levels of the aggressive style, have an immature quality to them. When operating from this place, you'll think or say things like "this person *never* listens to me" or "they always do" such and such. Others have hurt you, life is unfair, and now you're going to tip the scales in your favor and start getting yours.

This might sound bad and make you cringe to read — I mean, nice people don't think or act like this, do they? But actually, a little spark of this energy is sometimes exactly what is needed to get out of decades of passive submission and beta behavior. It can help you push back against the oppression of others, defy the pressure to over-accommodate others, and firm up overly soft and mushy boundaries. While staying at this level won't ultimately bring you the optimal relationships and success you seek in life, in small doses, it just might be exactly what the doctor ordered.

In level 8 of the aggressive style, the screws around the armor of your heart tighten, and now you not only feel entitled to get what you want, you feel enraged if someone stands in your way. The core communication to others is "I'm going to say it and you're going to take it." You are going to get what you want no matter what, and if someone hinders you, then you have a righteous reason for revenge.

This level of communication can happen in workplaces, families, friendships, or even with an intimate partner. This can be quite disorienting and confusing, especially to nice people, who are shocked that someone they love could be so harsh with them if they don't accommodate all their needs and desires. This pattern is the core of the classic dance of the relationship between the overly nice empath and the charming narcissist.

Someone coming at you from this level will often be very certain and congruent within themselves, and therefore sound confident and convincing. They can cause you to second guess yourself, dismiss your own internal warning signals, and end up giving and doing way more than you would in other situations.

It's absolutely essential to notice when someone is "coming at you hard" and instantly see it as a warning sign on your dashboard. Your internal impulse may be a fearful compulsion to accommodate them, give them what they want, and please them. However, unlike in a mutually beneficial assertive relationship, a person who regularly plays at **Level 8** will take and then just take some more.

The top of the scale of aggression is Level 9, in which someone's intent is to injure through a verbal attack, physical intimidation, threats and coercion, or physical violence. This level comes from a convoluted, distorted, or inverted perception of reality in which they are the victim of others who "make" them do violent things. For example, "I wouldn't have spent the last 45 minutes verbally berating you if you didn't make the mistake of paying that bill late."

At this level, other people's needs are not only irrelevant; other people are mere objects upon which someone projects their own inadequacies, pain, and self-hatred. This is the realm of abusive relationships, toxic workplace environments, and domestic violence. If you find yourself interacting with someone who's regularly playing at Level 9 in their communication, there's only one effective solution: **get out!** As safely and swiftly as possible.

All three levels of the aggressive style tend to downplay or outright deny the significance of other's needs', or even others as complete and complex beings just like ourselves. We tend to reduce others to a role (i.e., mother, sibling, boss) and then see them as "bad" because they're not doing that role right.

The aggressive style is an immature approach to relationships and life. It might seem dominant and powerful, and certainly can be scary, especially if threats or violence are involved, but it's anything but adult. It actually has much more of a resemblance to a four-year-old who pushes his two-year-old brother around when no one's watching. He gets what he wants, and gets to feel big and powerful for a few moments.

When operating in the aggressive style, the goal is not to connect with others, but rather to feel that sense of power and bigness. To be significant and right. To win. To have the fear and worthlessness that deep down is running their life pause for a brief moment while they feel a sense of righteous certainty.

CHAPTER 25

SHOW TEETH

Reading the above chapter, you may conclude that the aggressive style is bad news. You may even go so far as to strengthen the nice person programming that says: *anger is bad, and all those who feel or express anger are also bad.*

This rule might take on a new layer of sophistication, as it did with me for many years. Instead of simply saying, "I'm scared of anger," or, "I'm scared of conflict," or "I'm scared of the guilt and shame I feel when I express anger," we package the whole thing up to look better.

As an anger-phobic young man, I found the teachings of spirituality and new-age philosophy that encouraged forgiveness, turning the other cheek, and not letting things get to you particularly appealing. Thus, fighting back was bad. It showed you had too big of an ego and got hooked. If someone criticized, judged, ridiculed, or attacked me, the right thing to do was meditate it away. If I felt irritation, dislike, or judgment of someone else, that too was a sign of getting hooked by my ego. The best way to respond was to take the high road. Remain peaceful and not let them get to me.

It was all an act of course. One that fooled even myself. I wasn't really that peaceful, I was scared. I had loads of emotional-induced physical maladies including digestion problems, jaw tension, and chronic pain all over the place.

The truth is anger is useful. Anger can be good.

In our house we have two dogs — a little Australian shepherd and a gigantic german shepherd. The little guy is small, but scrappy. He especially doesn't like when other dogs get near his food. If our big bumbly german shepherd gets near something he's chewing on, he'll curl his lips and show his fangs. In dog speak, this means "back off buddy."

If you are trying to become more assertive and you think the assertive style is all peace and hugs and rainbows, your assertiveness will be significantly less effective at creating the relationships and life that you want.

Anger is a key fuel for assertiveness. It's part of the combustion that creates the power behind your communication. Without it, your attempts to assert yourself can be like a soft noodle. A dog with no fangs. In essence, someone who is easily ignored or walked over.

To gain your full strength and capacity in your assertive power, it starts with no one else involved. Just you and anger. You and the parts of yourself. When you are alone, do you let yourself feel the heat of anger? Do you go swimming in those tumultuous waters, letting them buffet you around in the storm for a little bit?

Or do you try to only remain peaceful and calm? Do you try to deny your anger or undermine the feeling with a list of reasons why you shouldn't feel it? Or do you tell yourself repeatedly that there's nothing to be upset about and to just drop it?

I have met many nice people who are drawn to mindfulness meditation because it promises the possibility of feeling angry and "remaining mindful." They interpret this as being in control at all times; their scary anger never overtakes them.

Of course, being able to let something go quickly might be a fantastic skill and just the thing to do at a given moment. But if that's the only approach you have, and going into anger makes you terrified because you imagine it will overtake you, disintegrate your relationships, and destroy your life, then you may need to expand your emotional repertoire.

Because when someone is interrupting you or trying to bully or shame you at work, it's time to show teeth. No, I don't mean sending them a disturbing package with a threatening letter and a severed toe in it, or smashing their windshield with a golf club in the parking garage. Or pounding your fist on the table in the meeting and shouting over them. Those purely aggressive styles only end up hurting you in the long run and are rarely effective at getting what you actually want.

But when you *do* open your mouth to challenge the treatment at work, your voice will have some heat on it. Your sense of frustration or anger can show. It can be seen in your body language and heard in your voice tone. Your body is saying loud and clear: *NO. I don't like this. I don't want this.*

In short, making contact with your anger makes the words you say match your energy, and your communication is fully congruent. This congruence makes you much more effective at getting your point across and being heard.

CHAPTER 26

THE FIRE

It's okay, allow yourself a little hate
Hatred is not so bad when directed at injustice
You can turn the other cheek, just don't turn the other way
— NOFX, *American Errorist*

Many clients I work with are open to the idea of feeling their anger more. In private. But the idea of letting any upset, irritation, or frustration show feels too scary or threatening. They want the anger to be private and the conflict to be watered down, calm, placid and peaceful.

While skillful assertiveness is made up of conversations rather than screaming, throwing objects or physical violence, it is not necessarily calm and placid. A direct conversation, even in a normal voice tone and volume, can be very uncomfortable, upsetting, or stimulating.

Ultimately, that is what is needed for you to become a freer, more authentic version of yourself. You must let yourself go more readily into conflict with other people. It's okay. You're allowed to get angry, upset, irritated, hurt, frustrated, repulsed, or enraged. In fact, sometimes, these are the most healthy responses to certain situations.

I hear so many stories from clients in conversations with friends, colleagues, or romantic partners that set off alarm bells in my head. Phrases such as:

"He told me I was a terrible mother and was unfit to be with my children."

"She said I was a selfish asshole for not wanting to spend time with her over the weekend."

"She threatened to text all our friends and tell them that I cheated on her, even though I never had."

In all of these cases, my clients felt scared and unsettled in these interactions. They left feeling confused, wondering if they were indeed unfit to parent, a bad and selfish friend, or at fault for not giving the other person what they were demanding.

When they would tell me about it, their tone would be composed and factual, as if they were reporting a news story. One thing all of them did not seem to have is anger... at least not initially. They felt guilty, responsible, concerned, scared, unsure, self-doubt, and many other feelings.

But they didn't seem to feel outraged or indignant. They didn't seem to have that alarm bell go off that said, "how dare you treat me this way?! That's unacceptable. I will not tolerate this!" Without that, toleration was their only option. In their minds, it was against the rules to challenge the other person or fight back. Heck, forget fighting back; it was against the rules to simply show their teeth, and be something other than submissive, deferring, and accommodating.

What I guided each of my clients to do, and what I am suggesting to you, is to give yourself permission to bare your fangs. This, my friend, is the fire. This fire that is inside of you right now is keeping you alive, vital, authentic, and congruent with your own nature. When you hold back, stuff your revulsion, and bend backward to accommodate unacceptable behavior, you smother this inner flame.

Do you know what I'm talking about? Can you feel how bad it feels to dampen that flame within? How awful is it to compromise who you are, sell yourself out, and be someone other than who you truly are, all to keep the peace?

You're allowed to have a wide variety of emotional reactions to the people and circumstances in your life. You're allowed to feel hurt, angry, upset, or disappointed. If someone does something inconsiderate, dismissive, or cruel, you're allowed to feel strong emotions of anger or revulsion.

None of this makes you a bad person or somehow less spiritual, mature, or enlightened. The maturity comes from your capacity to be aware of these reactions and have a wide range of options to choose from for your response.

To really hammer this point home, let me give you a some what absurd and shocking example. Imagine you were standing in a line along the sidewalk to order at a restaurant counter. As you stand there, chatting with a friend, a stranger walks up to you and slaps you across the face, loudly proclaiming, "We don't like your type around here, get out of this line."

What would you feel at this moment? Peaceful? Forgiving? Enlightened? If so, you may need to reduce your Valium dosage. A natural response to this would be confusion, anger, embarrassment, disgust, dislike, and outrage. Or, in other words, "What the f**k? How dare you treat me that way?"

While this example might seem extreme and obviously outrageous, how many people are enduring much worse treatment than this on a daily basis? Perhaps even in their intimate relationship? They tolerate escalating levels of disrespectful treatment, oppression, and abuse. And their inner fire becomes more and more covered with dirt and debris until it's just a little puff of smoke smoldering beneath the pile.

You might say, "But Aziz, I'm not in an abusive relationship" so I have nothing to feel upset about. Fair enough. Maybe it's not so extreme in your case. But are you never annoyed with anyone in your life? Does everyone always treat you with total kindness and respect?

Or are there moments in which someone seems to disregard you, talk over you, or dismiss your feelings or requests? While they may not be abusive by any means, do you have a fire inside that responds? A flame that gives you the permission and fuel to stand up for yourself, express your upset, request a new way of relating, or challenge an old pattern in a relationship?

Or is that fire buried under a big dirt pile with an "I'm super calm, spiritual, and easy-going" flag on the top of it?

CHAPTER 27

ABOVE THE BELT

Alright. Alright! I get it, Aziz. I gotta start speaking up for myself. If someone steps on my toes, I need to show my fangs, explode my inner fire and fight back, right?

Well, yes and no. It really depends on how you do it. "Yes" to feeling upset and having a healthy sense of permission to speak up for yourself. "No" to you can say and do whatever you want and others have to sit there and listen to you.

This chapter and the next will share more of the nuances to speaking up, and what tends to be most skillful, get the best responses, and build healthy relationships over the long-term.

What tends to go well in conflict is when you can take ownership of your feelings, express yourself with "I" language, and be aware that you are sharing your *interpretation* of whatever happened.

That was a dense sentence chalk full of wisdom. In fact, if you're into highlighting books as you read them, definitely highlight that last sentence. I'll also share more about what each one of those phrases mean.

Taking Ownership: When taking total ownership of your life, you decide that you are responsible for your choices, actions, and response to outcomes. Applied to relationships and communication, it can be summed up as this: *I know ultimately I am responsible for my feelings, I'm responsible to ask for what I want and need in relationships, and I'm responsible to bring up things that are bothering me directly to resolve them.*

"I" Language: You focus on your subjective experience rather than labeling the other person. You'd say things like "I'm feeling hurt" or "I'm angry," rather than "you don't care about me" or "you're a selfish jerk."

Aware of Your Interpretation: You remain aware that you are interpreting the events and other people's meanings and motives, rather than collapsing to a sense of total certainty that you are seeing it the one and only way it is. This awareness allows others to have a different perspective than your own. Instead of saying "You don't care about me," which is an interpretation, you might say something like, "When you didn't ask me how I was feeling after I got hurt, I imagine that means you don't care about me."

The two phrases in the sentence above might sound similar, but it makes a world of difference in the conversation. It helps the other person see what event you're referring to and what conclusion you came to. They might have a very different perspective of that event. When you share in this way, there's space for them to share their perspective and for both of you to learn.

If it's a more simplistic "You don't care about me" statement, it's hard to know exactly what you're referring to, and there's no space to interpret the situation in a different way. It also makes people prone to defend their viewpoint rather than being curious, discovering something new, and actually resolving the conflict.

What tends to not go well in conflict is blaming, tantruming, character attacks, ridicule or disdain, and being dismissive or defensive. While reading this list might sound obvious, in the moment of conflict, you may be engaging in one or more of these patterns without even knowing it.

In fact, just this morning, my wife brought up something that was upsetting her, and I reacted with some degree of defensiveness. Which, as you might expect, did not go very well. Why did I do that? I do write books about connection and communication; after all, shouldn't I be better at it than that?

It turns out these suboptimal patterns for conflict can be quite subtle and persist despite becoming more skilled in conflict. Because if I, or anyone, feel their sense of "goodness" being threatened, they will run one of these patterns. In other words, if you imagine the other person is saying, "you are bad," and part of you agrees that they are right, then you might feel shame and a threat to your sense of goodness or worthiness, so you will push back, counter, defend, dismiss, or do something else protective, perhaps without even knowing it.

To give you a sense of each of these, here's a brief description:

Blaming: The focus is on the other person and what they did or didn't do, rather than on your own feelings. Blame is often vague or generalized rather than focusing on a specific incident. Usually, when blaming, we're attached to a single perspective of what happened and what it means, and we get angry if someone tries to offer a different perspective. We're attached to being right, righteous, and superior. Blaming can be with direct statements such as "you always put yourself first" or rhetorical questions such as "Why do you always do that?" It can also be more subtle, manifesting as a slight tone of shaming disapproval or statements that seem like "I language" but are really blaming, such as "I don't feel appreciated by you."

Tantruming: A hot tantrum includes explosive emotion, yelling, ranting, dramatic gestures, lots of blaming, and hurtful statements. A cold tantrum involves throwing up your hands and saying "fine, I don't care!" and walking away in a manner that shows that you absolutely do care. Or being pouty, sighing, and huffle-puffing around the house for hours as you give someone the silent treatment and the stink eye for a week.

Character Attacks: You generalize beyond the specific incident and make a conclusion about how someone is overall. You label them in your head and out loud with an adjective that generally means they're bad, such as selfish, narcissistic, mean, careless, reckless, immature, stupid, etc.

Ridicule or Disdain: Here, you attempt to get rid of the offending viewpoint or emotions by mocking or deriding them. They're so absurd for even existing, and the person having them is even more absurd! It may involve mocking through magnification, in which you amplify their emotion to a comical degree by saying something like, "Oh are you sad? Poor baby." Disdain doesn't have the same mocking quality. It's more straight-up disgust and contempt that someone would even have that desire, thought, request, emotion, or behavior.

Dismissive or Defensive: The essence of this strategy can be summed up in the timeless children's taunt: "I'm rubber, you're glue, whatever you say bounces off me and stick to you." Basically they can't pin anything on you because you didn't do anything. And their perceptions of whatever happened are wrong, distorted, overly emotional, or unrealistic. When listening to what the other person shares, your main objective is to find flaws, inconsistencies, and other inaccuracies so you challenge them, thus undermining the validity of the original upset. In other words, you're like rubber.

Ultimately, all of these patterns come out of the need to defend the self. They emerge when you sense the lurking specter of shame is nearby and could descend upon you at any moment. Shame is that awful feeling that you are bad, wrong, icky, unworthy, and wretched, making you unlovable and unredeemable. It's the lowest energy of human emotion and a place that no one wants to go.

Of course, the other person might not actually be saying you are bad, unlovable, and irredeemably wretched. They might just be saying they don't like the way you make coffee. But the more prone you are to feeling shame, the harder communication becomes and the worse your relationships suffer.

A major component of the healing work I do in my group coaching programs is to help clients liberate themselves from a recurring sense of shame and inferiority. This makes them not only feel much happier and lighter, it also does wonders for their communication.

If you'd like to interrupt this pattern of shame and self-implosion, I highly recommend reading my book "*On My Own Side,*" which is a deep study of getting right with yourself and celebrating who you truly are in this life.

And now for a quick recap:

Above The Belt	Below The Belt
Taking Ownership	Blaming
Using "I" Language	Tantruming
Aware of Your Interpretation	Character Attacks
	Ridicule or Disdain
	Dismissive or Defensive

For optimal results in relationships and life, when communicating your upset, keep it above the belt.

CHAPTER 28

3 LEVELS OF SKILLFUL COMMUNICATION

There are a lot of nuances here that can make speaking up seem hard or impossible to do "just right." And maybe it is. Maybe human beings and our communication are inherently messy, and there is no such thing as speaking up perfectly (or doing anything perfectly, for that matter!).

Besides, often your desire to do it perfectly is just another form of avoiding conflict or discomfort. You imagine that if you just said and did everything just right, then no one would ever get upset, or say something back that you didn't like, or withdraw. But these outcomes are some of the inevitable possibilities that can occur when you stop hiding and trying to be liked and instead start showing up and trying to know others and be known. It's a completely different game. And as with all games, while you can't ever become perfect, you sure can become more skillful. To help you understand what that might look or sound like in your life as you speak up more, I'd like to give you three examples of speaking up at different levels of skillfulness. We'll call them levels one, two, and three.

After each level, you'll get a chance to reflect on how it feels to hear it, and what makes it more or less skillful. This can help you further refine your abilities as you practice speaking up more and more.

Now, I'm going to repeat myself here because it's such an exceptionally important point for you to get from this book. **The only way you are going to get better is by speaking up. A lot**. More than a few times. More than once in a long while only when the situation becomes so intolerable that you're forced to.

Don't use being skillful as another reason to hold back and hide, telling yourself: *I'll wait to speak up later when I'm better at it.* There is only one way to get better at it. Just like all skills, you must practice regularly. So get started today. It's okay to be a little bumbling or clunky, a little (or significantly) unskillful. You'll learn quickly and become a master in no time.

Here's the scenario I'll demo with, which just happened several days ago. My wife and I had a weekend away from our boys, which is a rare occurrence indeed. It just so happened that during this weekend, a friend of ours was holding her annual gathering out in the woods for her birthday that involved three days of connecting and listening to bass in the woods. Score.

On Saturday night at this little festival gathering, I was having a great time connecting with my wife and some close friends I hadn't seen in a while, as well as some new friends, all while immersed in an ocean of bass. It doesn't get any better than that.

At one point, I excused myself to go back to our little camper van to refill our water bottles. I left the main area and walked along the dark path for about five minutes until I reached our van, where I hopped inside and refilled the water bottles. While alone, I realized there were several messages from friends that I hadn't gotten around to yet who I wanted to connect with. I began sending messages and recording a few audios.

Apparently more time had passed than I realized, and my wife emerged from the darkness to be illuminated by the warm lights of the van cabin.

Okay. That's the setup. It might seem like no big deal, and it isn't. But little things like this happen all day long in our relationships, both personal and professional. Little moments of missed communication, perceived slights, and potentials for hurt or upset.

The situation is less important than the ways you might communicate. If you were Candace, what would you say in that situation? What would it mean to you that I was gone for longer than I had implied? What would you have concluded about my absence?

These questions are essential to ask because skillful communication doesn't start with what comes out of your mouth. It starts with what goes on in your mind. **Level 1, or unskillful communication**, starts with strong conclusions in the mind about what something means. There's a sense of certainty that this is correct and no other perspective is possibly more true. You're "right" from the beginning and unwilling to genuinely question that. There's a hardness with that rightness, and now your communication will most likely be about making the other person wrong, admitting that they're wrong, and then apologizing to you to atone. Upon receiving the apology, if you get it, you then allow yourself to soften and let them back into your heart.

Can you see how this is less skillful, even before I've demonstrated what someone might actually say from this place. Skillful communication is all about where you come from, not the exact words that you say.

Let's say you concluded that my absence means that I don't care about you, or that you are not worthy of my time, or that you are an annoying tag along who isn't really that fun to be around, or some other self-critical or negative story. From this painful place of hurt and imagined worthlessness, you might don your armor of rightness and pride and say:

"Where were you? Why have you been here so long?"

Your tone might be sharp or accusatory. I might perceive that and attempt to connect by saying, "Oh, I'm sorry! I got wrapped up in responding to messages and didn't notice how much time had passed."

But that might not be enough to soften the armoring. You might have an urge to prove the story in your mind is true. *You really don't care about me...* And it's not just this moment — it's a hundred other moments that prove you don't care about me. And, if you really want to swing into unskillful territory, you can say how selfish and self-centered they are. How they only care about themselves and how terrible that is.

When we're being unskillful, our main outcome isn't to reconnect. It's to cause pain. We're already feeling pain from our conclusions, and we then attempt to cause pain in others. Once we have done so sufficiently, then we can soften and reopen our hearts.

This isn't bad or wrong or evil. It's just unskillful. And we all do it at times. To really see this, face it, and change it to become more skillful in our communication is a humbling practice of honesty with ourselves and others, a practice of vulnerability, and being able to see just how quickly and automatically we can armor our hearts.

Let's talk about **Level 2 communication**. You, and everyone else who's actively improving their communication abilities, must pass through this level. In Level 2, you're definitely taking more responsibility and communicating with more openness, but the mental conclusions and stories still have so much momentum to them, that the outcome is often similar to level 1.

In Level 2, you are more self-aware. In the example above regarding my disappearing on you, you notice that after I've been gone for longer than you expected that you start to feel uncomfortable. You may be aware that you feel lonely or fear being separated and not being able to find me for the rest of the night. You also notice the conclusions about not being worth my time, a bother, and so forth.

In Level 2, you are often aware of the painful conclusions and more vulnerable feelings underneath, but the old painful stories about your worth still feel so true that it's hard to let them go.

Communication from this place might reveal more, such as "When you didn't come back, I felt worried that you might not come back and we'd be apart all night," which is vulnerable and connecting. But then it's followed up with much of the same Level 1 stuff, perhaps without the character attacks. Together, it might sound something like this:

"Oh, there you are! Whew! When you didn't come back, I felt worried that you might not come back and we'd be apart all night. When you leave like that it makes me feel small and worthless. I hate it when you do that! In the future don't ever do that again."

How does it feel to be on the receiving end of that communication? The vulnerability is definitely connecting and often opens the door for compassion. What keeps this from being fully skillful, however, is that you are still locked in a perspective of how it is. You're not taking ownership of your own insecurities and conclusions, and instead, you're trying to control outer circumstances and other people so you don't have to face uncomfortable feelings that, most likely, existed long before you met this partner.

For example, if you feel jealous every time your partner talks with someone attractive, and then you try to resolve that situation by controlling your partner, then you're not actually addressing the real issue. Because you felt insecure before this partner and you will after. It exists independently of them. They are not the *cause* of your pain. Can you see that?

To reach Level 3 and the highest level of skill in communication, you must take total ownership. That means acknowledging *my insecurities are mine*. When you do something and I conclude I'm not lovable, that is my own story that I've had since, well, forever. It's my responsibility to take ownership for it when I share it with you. It's not your fault. You're not to blame for "making me" feel that way.

When I help clients become less nice and speak up more, I often see them rapidly grow from Level 1 to Level 2. But then they will often stall out in Level 2 for a while because they have a hard time seeing what they're missing. The key is to see that skillful communication is not about the words you use, it's about where you are coming from.

As long as I'm making you responsible for poking my insecurities, fabricating the story that you created this feeling in me, then blame will come out, even in subtle emotional or energetic ways, which will hinder the impact of your communication.

So what does **Level 3** look and sound like? Well, for this we must start again from where you come from. Let's say you become aware of the longing to be with me, the fear that you might not find me for the rest of the night, and then a painful feeling of being unwanted or unloved.

Skillful communication starts with awareness of all this, and a genuine care and compassion for what you discover. In **Level 2**, you still blame yourself for your insecurities, you don't like those parts of you, and so you push them down and don't fully reveal them to others. You dislike yourself for having those parts and then you pass the blame hot potato to the other person. *I'm not bad, you're bad!*

In order to truly be skillful in honesty and communication, you must notice all these parts of yourself and meet them with true curiosity and compassion. I teach this in depth in my book, *"On My Own Side: Transform Self-Criticism and Doubt Into Permanent Self-Worth and Confidence."*

Then you don't need to make any parts of you wrong, or any parts of others wrong. You can communicate with much more clarity, simple directness, and vulnerability.

Level 3 would sound something like this: "Oh! There you are. I'm so relieved to see you. When you didn't come back I felt this pang of fear that you'd be gone all night and I wouldn't find you until tomorrow... Then I felt that part of me that feels like she's not worthy of love and who others won't want to be around. It was so painful!"

Can you feel the difference in this, as you imagine receiving this from a friend or a partner? My wife actually said something very similar to this to me when she found me that night. My response was one of surprise, love, and compassion.

"Oh no! I'm sorry, my love. I just got in here and started responding to one person and then lost track of time. Aww, sweetheart!" I said as I wrapped her in a big hug.

If she had blamed me harshly or subtly, I may still have moved towards her, but it would have been tinged with some level of fear or shame. Instead, her skillful, vulnerable communication evoked a response of genuine care and compassion in me, which is what Level 3 communication often does.

This doesn't mean that you can't have boundaries, preferences, or requests. After saying this, she might say, "When we separate at places like this, I'd like to have a better plan for meeting up" or "in the future, if you're going to possibly be gone longer, can you tell me so I'm aware of that?"

This is going back to our good old friend _____. That's a pop-quiz by the way. What is she doing here in this hypothetical example? She's taking a _____ that she has in her mind and attempting to turn it into an _____ between us.

No, I will not give you the answers. But if you don't know what goes in that blank, you may want to jump back to chapter 18 for a minute to review.

CHAPTER 29

SAY NO

"So what do you think?" she asked as she held up the drawing.

"Yeah... that looks good," I said, only pausing for a moment.

"Okay, great!" she replied. "Give me a few minutes to transfer it to tracing paper and we'll begin."

Within several minutes she had the tracing paper pressed against my skin, transferring the outline of a large tattoo against my shoulder and upper arm. A tattoo that I didn't even like that much. But what could I do, say no?

My kids are fascinated by this story. They ask me to tell it again and again and giggle with surprise and delight.

"Why didn't you tell her you didn't like it, daddy?"

"Why didn't you ask her to change it?"

These are great questions. Why don't you tell someone you don't like something? Why don't you ask someone to change the way they're doing something? Why don't you say "no" freely and easily at the moment?

The answer, my friend, is what I call "the override". This is when you receive a subtle — or not so subtle — signal from your body, heart, or intuition that tells you that you don't like something, but you use some quick mental maneuver to ignore the signal and proceed ahead.

This can happen so quickly and automatically that you don't even fully notice the inner signal. You have some standard, boiler-plate override thoughts that swoop in to keep the whole show moving forward. Thoughts such as:

- *I don't want to be offensive, a burden, a bother, or high-needs;*
- *I don't want to upset them;*
- *I should be more open-minded;*
- *I should be more flexible and go with the flow;*
- *I shouldn't care so much.*

Or, the granddaddy of all override thoughts: *whatever, it's no big deal.* Except it is a big deal, especially when it's a freaking tattoo that you're going to put on your body for the rest of your life! Or when it's a person that you continue to date even though you feel done. Or when a friend or sibling dominates the conversation and you feel suffocated and like you want to scream, but you don't boldly speak up. Those are big deals.

Because what you feel and want matters. What you don't want matters. How you want things to change matters. You matter.

Stop discounting your feelings and yourself and downplaying your inner signals. Stop keeping yourself in situations that are bad, okay, or even "Pretty good, I guess" by hitting that override command for months or years. That's your life passing you by, not fully lived.

What do you say to yourself to override? Become very familiar with your override phrases. Otherwise they will slip by, unnoticed, continuing to control your words and behaviors.

Of course, upon closer examination, you can see they are all BS! It isn't about being open-minded, flexible, or easy going. It's about avoiding direct conversation, disagreement, or conflict. It's about keeping everything as smooth as possible, perpetuating the idea that others are fragile and volatile creatures who will simultaneously be crushed and freak out just because you told them no or shared your preference that might slightly differ from theirs.

Why didn't I say "No" to that tattoo artist and ask her to tweak the drawing? Because I was too damn nice, that's why! More specifically, because I didn't want to hurt her feelings by telling her that her art wasn't good enough. I also didn't want her to be irritated or upset with me because I believed I couldn't handle that.

Looking back, the entire situation is utterly baffling to me. My ability now to quickly speak up and say what I like and don't like and how I want things to change is radically different. Now, I would also have her tweak it until I loved it, even if that meant many iterations. If she got fed up with making changes, then I would pay her for her time and go find another tattoo artist. I wouldn't feel bad, or guilty, or scared. She's a person providing a service in the world and I am paying her for that service. I want the tattoo to be awesome, especially as it is kind of a big commitment.

That's what I've noticed in my clients who've grown radically and feel like a different version of themselves. They are shocked at the hundreds of ways they invalidated themselves and didn't say things that now seem so simple to say.

It's not because they're way smarter now. Or that they have spent a decade mastering conflict negotiation. All they've done is simply remove the fear and avoidance of speaking up. They decided to stop hiding and take the leap. They've proven to themselves, by upgrading their beliefs and taking consistent bold action, that they can speak up, others can handle it, and so can they.

One of my client's, Eric, runs a highly successful business online. In order to get there, he had to say "No" to his dad, as he worked for the family business. His dad told him that he "wouldn't make it in this online business nonsense" and that he would fail, which was apparently the exact form of motivation to get Eric going at hyper speed.

Eric put in the time, energy, study, and focus needed to make his business start, survive, and ultimately thrive. He became willing to fail, which he did numerous times along the way. He also became willing to say no.

He shared one moment with me that felt like a total turning point in his life. He had a vendor who quoted him one price and then, right before delivery, told him a new price, which was substantially more than what they had agreed upon. In the past, he would have overridden his inner signal of aversion or dislike and just paid the difference — not anymore.

He didn't message or email the vendor. He called them. Not just a phone call either, but a video call. Talk about approach. He spoke with them and told them that this was unacceptable and he wanted to work with companies that kept their word. If they could not do this, he no longer wanted to work with them.

Apparently, one of their employees had made a mistake when giving the quote. Not only that, but Eric could hear her in the background, crying. Yep, I'm not making that up. She was audibly crying in the background. When he shared that in our group coaching call, other members were scrunching up their faces in confusion and alarm, clearly able to see how important it was for him to speak up regardless of her reaction. It's always easier to be less nice and more real when you're focused on someone else.

But Eric was the one at the moment, being the Not-Nice Guy, making this poor woman cry. Even though a wave of guilt started to overtake him, he stayed in the moment, knowing that a life of not wanting to make others uncomfortable had kept him stuck, frustrated, and not living his best life. So he stayed in it until the vendor agreed to keep the original rate.

After clearing up any remaining guilt on his next group coaching call, he emerged a new man. He walked differently, talked differently, and smiled more. It was as if a multi-decade energetic and emotional burden had been released. His face even changed, and now his skin and eyes look younger and more vibrant than when I first met him.

When you are willing to face your fears and walk through the fire of saying "No" and sticking to it, instead of dying, you will actually burn away the limitations that have been holding you back all these years.

CHAPTER 30

PERMISSION TO DISAPPOINT

One fine summer day, I was laying on the mossy ground in a forest near my house. A mere hour ago, I'd been sitting in my office with the door open. The gentle breeze, sparkling sunshine, and warm, final-days-of-summer air, rich with the scent of ripe blackberries was simply too much to resist. I turned off my computer, grabbed my daypack (which was always by the door and ready for such spontaneous adventures), woke up one of my dogs and set out down the road.

There I lay amongst the sticks and moss and leaves, using my backpack as a pillow, looking up at the tall doug fir trees gently swaying and creaking in the soft breeze. Sometimes life is so sweet it makes me ache inside in the most painful, delightful, mysterious sort of way. *It doesn't get any better than this.*

But it wasn't all peace, love and rainbows. I noticed I had a nagging background emotion. Some sort of mucky mixture of anxiety and guilt. It felt heavy and draining and produced a tense feeling in my ribs. Remember that background radiation? Yep, there it was.

What was it? Did I forget something? Did I have a meeting that I blew off without realizing it?

And then it hit me like a lightning bolt of instant clarity. I wasn't missing anything. This feeling is not due to some specific oversight on my part. It's... always... there.

I would sum this unpleasant background hum as this: *Somewhere, right now in this very moment, someone is disappointed with me.* This gem of a thought then leads to an incessant, ruminative searching of the mind, looking for who it might be, like a disorganized, drunk attorney searching through piles of papers on his messy desk. "I know it's here somewheres... where did I put that brief!"

Only that day, there was nothing to find. But that was okay. I knew my mind would simply fill in the gap by imagining how someone, somewhere *could* be upset with me right now.

Can you relate to this? Are you doing this? Perhaps you're doing this even right now?

Have you not done something for someone? Gotten back to that email? Texted your sister back or called your mom recently? What about that thing you promised to help your friend with, or that project that you're overdue on, or your mom's best friend's cousin's wedding gift that you forgot to get? (How could you!)

And here's the worst part. The more confident you become, and the more you put yourself out there, the more people you touch and become connected with. That means there's even more people to disappoint!

And that's how it had gone for me, for years. Decades. Centuries. Well, maybe not that long, but certainly much of my life. I don't want to disappoint people. I'm afraid of disappointing people. The feeling that occurs when I think, or hear about, or see someone disappointed with me or because of something I did or didn't do is excruciating.

It has led to all kinds of issues of overcommitting, agreeing to too many things, and even staying in bad relationships because I didn't want to feel that wretched feeling. Because my nice programming taught me that when I disappoint someone, I don't just feel bad, I am bad. A classic shame smoothie.

But something was different that sunny summer day. Somehow the entire pattern came into my awareness — the thoughts and feelings, how long I'd been doing it, and most importantly, that I was the one creating it. It was a funny little dance that I was participating in, because as the old saying goes, it takes two to tango.

The steps of this old dance go something like this: *If you are disappointed in me, then I must have done or not done something, and that's bad. Who knows if you have crazy expectations or whether we had an agreement or not. That's irrelevant. Your expectations are my rules.*

Now I must discover what I did wrong and fix it as swiftly as possible, through apology, making amends, or giving whatever is needed. We'll know it worked when you feel appeased and all is once again right and well with the world.

Yuck. Yuck to this dance. Yuck to that lock-step, rigid, confining, restricting, constricting, life-suffocating dance. Let's do something different, shall we? Let's think outside the box, outside the old rules, outside the cultural field and how "it is" and "should be." Let's think for ourselves and be the powerful creator beings that we are. You and me, right now.

So, that afternoon I decided something different. I decided I was willing to disappoint.

I'll pause for a minute for the fanfare.

Okay, let's try this; say out loud right now:

"I am willing to disappoint."

Come on, now, say it like you mean it.

"I am willing to disappoint! Yayyy!"

Be sure to say the "yayyy" part, that's very important (note the extra "y's" that means you have to extend it.)

When I said it — out loud to the trees and the forest and my dog who was restlessly pacing about and guarding me from mountain lions — I meant it. I claimed it. I let that heavy ball of tar-like tension release from my ribs straight into the soil below me.

Upon claiming this, extraordinary, delightful things unfolded. We will have to wait and see what occurs for you, but for me I had a flurry of new thoughts and realizations. The flood gates were open and freedom was rushing in.

You can feel disappointed and that has nothing to do with me.

I repeated this thought over and over again as I thought about various people in my life: clients, friends, parents, my wife and children. At first, it seemed too far. Like I wanted to qualify it by saying that if you feel disappointed that might not have anything to do with me. I mean after all, maybe I did do something that let them down and need to acknowledge, and blah blah blah.

Nope. I cut out all the verbiage and went straight to the essence, slicing through layers of over-responsibility.

You can try it now if you like. Take several slow, deep breaths, letting the air fill your torso and expand your lower ribs and back. As you breathe, think about several people in your life who come to mind and gently repeat: *You can feel disappointed and that has nothing to do with me.*

Let this settle and see how you feel. You might just feel 1,000 pounds lighter.

If your mind is resisting this, convincing you that disappointing others is dangerous and taking you one step closer to the dark side and death and ruin, then that's okay too. This chapter might be a time-release kinda thing that you can come back to after reading this book, or maybe even in six months when you're reading this thing again.

If you'd like more, you can continue the same process of gentle, deep breaths as you read and repeat the following little poem. You can even commit it to memory if you like, using it as a powerful tool of liberation whenever the need arises in your life.

You can want something from me.
And that has nothing to do with me.
I release you.
I release me.

CHAPTER 31

SAYING NO TO HELPING OTHERS

*O*h my God. Now he's gone too far.

I mean, it's one thing to say no to someone's preference, or to tell a vendor you want something different. Heck, it's probably okay to even say no to dating someone or staying in a relationship. But saying no to your elderly mother? Saying no to a depressed friend? Saying no to someone who needs your help? That's taking it too far! How selfish, how mean, how wrong!

You know, Aziz, this is what's wrong with the world today. Too many selfish people who only think of themselves. How rude. What has the world come to!

I find people like to simplify things to try and make sense of "the world" and come up with explanations as to why it's this way or that way. As if they could know about all humanity and all humans and all the nuances of their situations. Usually, when someone speaks like this, they are not illuminating anything about the world but revealing something about themselves. They are sharing their rules and preferences about how things "should" be.

How about I tell you a quick story and you tell me what you think.

One of my clients, Samantha, recently shared a challenge in the weekly meeting of my confidence mastermind group. She'd been a member for slightly over one year and in that time had made massive progress in finding her core self-esteem, taking risks, being more direct and assertive, and creating new and deeper friendships.

Now she was bumping up against a challenge that struck her to the core and challenged her niceness to a whole new level. She had an aging mother who lived all alone. She didn't get out of the house for a month and found it hard to shop or prepare her own food.

Samantha, being the good daughter, was willing to help her mother out. She'd bring groceries several times per week, after her long work day, before she came home to take care of her own teenage daughter.

Sometimes, her mother would make special requests for certain restaurant takeout. Samantha, being the good daughter, would oblige. As she didn't go out much, her mother also struggled with loneliness and a sense of social disconnection. She liked to spend time with Samantha and would ask her to stay longer, talk with her, or do things for her around the house. Samantha, who found it very hard to say no in these instances, would do what felt like the right thing and stay with her mother, talk with her, and help her as much as she could.

So what do you think? Is Samantha doing the right thing? If she did anything less, would that be bad? If she were to change the arrangement and sometimes say no to her mother, would that be part of what makes the world so bad and selfish these days?

It sure seems more complex than that to me.

Oh, but there's more. The plot thickens. Samantha has a brother who also lives in the same city who does way less. He drops off groceries for his mom, but doesn't stay there long, and when he does, it's only about a third of the time, leaving the lion share of the care for Samantha.

Samantha even offered her mother the opportunity to stay with her and her daughter in their house to make the care easier, but her mother didn't like that for she wanted her own place.

So there you have it. Mother needs daughter. Good daughter does what is needed, regardless of what she wants or what the impact is on her life, right?

That's how Samantha had been living, and anything else to her felt selfish, bad, and wrong. It didn't help that when she was a girl, her mother would tell her not to go play with friends because that would be "mean to leave your mother all alone."

I know this situation is tricky and many different people will have many different opinions about it. But I don't care about their opinions. I care about yours. And if this were my life, I'd care about mine.

There are many situations in life that are just plain challenging and it's hard to find a simple, easy way to meet everyone's needs and desires perfectly. Nice people generally try to simplify the equation by removing their own desires and just doing what others request or want. But, as you've probably observed, this might simplify your choices of what to do, but it certainly doesn't simplify your emotions or inner world.

In this case, Samantha was internally disturbed by it all. She felt trapped. She felt guilty if she imagined doing anything less, but at the same time, she was just barely getting by, had no time for self-care, and her social connections were atrophied due to a lack of time to nourish them. Her life was being put on hold so she could be a good daughter and "do the right thing."

But is it the right thing? Is there just one right thing? According to who is it the right thing? Her mother? What would "they" say? What you learned growing up? Are other options also potentially "right" or valid?

This is what I began to explore with Samantha. Not that I had the exact solution for her and her family, but I knew that more options were available and that exploring them did not make her a bad person. In fact, they are an essential part of her taking care of herself and living a life that is fully her own.

I also knew that whatever she chose would be right for her, even if it disappointed her mother. At first we explored the low-hanging fruit of simply spending a bit less time at her mother's house so she could get home earlier and have some time for her own daughter and to take care of herself. "What about only coming by once per week instead of two or three times?" I asked.

As you can imagine, there are dozens of new arrangements and possibilities. The problem is not finding new alternatives, the problem is the emotional zap Samantha gets when she explores these options, or even worse, if she were to choose one of them.

For her, the biggest obstacle was imagining her poor mother, all alone each evening, no one there to talk to, suffering all by herself. I'll admit it's a tragic vision and no wonder Samantha was hurting about it.

But is that Samantha's responsibility? What if Samantha didn't meet her mother's social needs as much? What would her mother do?

Well… how hungry for connection is she? Would she start talking to her neighbors? Would she go down to the town center to attend an event, or play in a bingo night, or find other ways to engage with others?

Is it possible that by meeting her mother's need for connection that Samantha was blocking the very impetus for her mom to go do something to address it?

Of course we're only talking about Samantha and her mom here, right? Not you or me…

Do you treat other people as if they are helpless victims who are incapable of caring for themselves? Unless you are dealing with an infant or someone who is so incapacitated they cannot think or function independently, then most likely you're taking on too much.

You are creating a fantasy in which you are the only one who can meet this person's needs. And in order to be a good person, you should/must do whatever is needed, regardless of what you want.

I've seen clients feel unable to leave a relationship they know is over because it would "Devastate my partner." They imagine their partner will never find anyone again, being traumatized by being abandoned.

This might sound like a caring and loving concern, but is it really true? It sure has you in the role of savior or hero, which might feel good temporarily, but it's an illusion that is deceiving both of you.

The truth is my client's partner is a powerful creator, as is Samantha's mother. Often it takes adverse circumstances or someone not coming to save us for us to harness our latent power and act on it. Determination, transforming energy, and grit all arise out of feelings of helplessness and hopelessness.

It turns out saying no might just be the best form of help you can give to someone.

CHAPTER 32

ASK UNAPOLOGETICALLY

"I feel so needy," Walt said.

"Just to clarify, is neediness bad?" I asked.

"Yes, definitely bad. It's pathetic," said Walt

"Okay," I chuckled. "Worse than bad!"

"Yeah, being needy is completely repulsive."

"I see." I paused for a moment, then said, "well, you did ask for something that you want. It feels important to you, like something you'd need to really thrive in this relationship."

"Yeah…" Walt agreed, begrudgingly.

"You've done relationships as the nice guy who pretends to have no needs, who just accepts whatever he gets, and that didn't work for you."

"That's right," he affirmed.

"So now you're doing something different and asking for the things that are important to you. But you're not sure if she's on board and is willing and available for that in your relationship."

"Right." At this point, Walt saw his predicament and looked somewhat miserable.

I continued speaking to Will, but also to every single other person who was attending the group call that evening. "This, right here, is the work. This is the process of growth, my friend. You challenge your conditioning, act counter to how you 'should be' in order to keep love and prove to yourself that another way is possible. This process is uncomfortable, and honestly, is sometimes agonizing. But it's the only way I know of to completely transform your way of being in the world. While it might seem 'bad' because it's painful, you can also view it as a form of purification. It's the fire that is burning away all the rules and patterns that don't serve you, that have burdened and confined you for years. All the ways of being in the world that are not truly you, that are false, fake. A fire that burns away all that is not you."

~

So… what is your reason for not fully, boldly, regularly, and unapologetically asking for what you want?

Perhaps your mind generates a dozen reasons…

I'll appear needy, they will feel burdened, they'll say "no" and that will be painful, I'll look weak, I'm asking for too much, I'm being selfish or greedy or (insert other synonym for "bad" here).

I could go on, and I'm sure you could too. What do you tell yourself to stop yourself from asking freely from others around you? It's good to become aware of your stories because all it takes is buying one of them to stop you dead in your tracks.

But underneath all these seemingly varied fears about asking for what you want, it all boils down to one story, one fear.

If I ask for what I want, I'll lose love or connection.

Can you see this? You can find your way there by simply following whatever fears you have about asking to their root with a simple inquiry that goes like this. Say your fear and then ask yourself, "then what will happen?"

For example:

If I ask for what I want, I'll appear needy.

=> Then what will happen?

The other person won't like me.

=> Then what?

They'll feel totally repulsed.

=> Then what?

They won't want to date me anymore.

I'm asking for too much.

=> If you're asking for too much, then what will happen?

Others at work will see me as demanding and a burden.

=> Then what will happen?

My supervisor will get frustrated with me and dislike me.

=> Then what?

I'll get fired or let go.

Do you see how it works? You can take one of your fears and try it out for yourself. See where it leads you. Most likely, it will lead to some sort of end of the connection, or at least the person being upset and withdrawing from you if they don't outright leave.

What's going on here? You're telling yourself that asking directly for what you want is offensive, bad, threatening, etc. Let's just go with that for a minute and see where it's coming from and where it's taking you.

The core underlying rule here is that you shouldn't have needs or wants that conflict with others. The old "have to needs" strategy. Where did you pick that one up? Most likely childhood, when you had bad experiences with having needs or advocating for them.

Now before you conclude that your parents are horrible monsters, let me explain. I used to think parents were meanies who should have been more patient and loving with their kids. Until I had my own. And then I realize that they can be a relentless freight train of pressure, advocating for their demands. They will ask, demand, cry, plead, bargain, negotiate, act out, freak out, threaten, apologize, make outlandish promises of what they will do, try and sneak it, steal it, lie about it, blame someone else… and that's all before lunch!

Holy cow, it's a lot. Now I'm sure you weren't like this because you were a little angel. But seriously, if you didn't act like this as a kid, it's probably because you already observed or intuitively picked up that you couldn't safely do that in your home environment. Either the parental impatience and disapproval were too unpleasant, or you felt the stress and overwhelm in your parents and didn't want to cause more upset in them.

So, you came up with a great solution. Erase your needs. No needs, no burden. No upset, no disapproval = no problems.

While this may have worked in a certain sense as a child, it certainly doesn't work in relationships, careers, or life. And as an adult, it's a downright terrible strategy.

You can see that right? I mean if I were to ask you to give advice to a friend who never asks for anything, subtly hints at what they want, and then feels guilty about it, what would you say to them? Wouldn't you encourage them to speak up and ask for what they want? Wouldn't you see their wants and needs as important?

I imagine you would. Because you know what works in the world. The problem is that what works also clashes with your old nice person programming. And to challenge that programming and start boldly asking is, well, uncomfortable.

That's it.

Every story about it, all your predictions, all the justifications and excuses are there to protect you from the emotional discomfort of just asking more.

The truth is that asking is not dangerous. It doesn't cause people to turn on you, attack you, or abandon you suddenly. What it does do, however, is let others know the real you, including what you really desire. This feels vulnerable, doesn't it? To be seen and known?

It's what we all want, and yet it feels so raw and wide open and out of control that we actually push it away despite craving it deep down.

If I hide those needs and play the role of a low-maintenance nice person then maybe you'll stick with me because I didn't put you out too much. That sure sounds like a recipe for an extraordinary love, doesn't it?

But if you choose to take the risk and let yourself and your needs be known, passing through the spooky forest of vulnerability where you could be pounced on by a cougar or otherwise hurt, you'll discover something magical...

People want to give you what you want!

Others in your life care about you. They want to know what lights you up. They will often say "yes," or do what they can to accommodate your needs and desires.

This isn't just with a partner or lover, and not even with your friends. This includes your workplace, with colleagues, and even at the discount tire shop.

When you approach people with warmth and openness, sharing what you want and why, they frequently respond with curiosity and a desire to help.

If this sounds like some bizarro fairy tale and like I'm living in a different universe than you, then, well, you might be right. Because you and I don't live in "the" reality. There is no singular reality. You and I, and every other human on this planet, we each inhabit our own reality.

Now before we go down some deep philosophical rabbit hole, I know we can all agree on simple objects: that's a tree, there's a car. The concrete world is very simple to describe and share. But humans don't live in the concrete world. We live in a world of emotion, meaning, good, bad, right and wrong.

Is that tree pretty? Is that a good car? Now we're no longer in the same reality. We each can have wildly different perspectives and meanings about what's happening, what's valuable, what's good or bad, right or wrong.

In my reality people often seek to help me get what I want. Knowing this, I approach them with warmth, connection, and an idea that we're going to solve this problem together.

If you are tense inside, bracing for them to reject, dismiss, or shame you, and feeling guilty because you believe it's wrong to ask or receive, then you inhabit a very different reality.

Which reality do you want to live in? Maybe it's time to relocate?

How?

Ask more!

Ask boldly and you just might get what you want...

PART IV

AN AUTHENTIC LIFE

CHAPTER 33

ONCE AND FOR ALL?

"All good?" Doug asked me as I sat in the driver seat.

"Yeah!" I replied enthusiastically.

Only I didn't feel enthusiastic on the inside. I felt a little tight and unsure. *Did I really want this?*

It was an unusually warm November afternoon that happened to be my birthday, and I was sitting in the driver seat of a small utility vehicle. In case you don't know what those are, which I didn't before I began my country-living lifestyle a scant 12 months ago, think of a golf cart on steroids: it's got all terrain wheels, four-wheel drive, and a dump bed to haul gravel, wood, and carry out all your macho duties around the land. Pretty sweet, huh?

Well, at that moment something felt off… *Was it too big for the trails around our land? It was awfully slow. It had no power steering, and why did the exhaust stink so much more than any other vehicle or tool I'd used?*

But I didn't voice any of these concerns or even show that I was uncertain. Why? Because I was afraid of Doug! Let me explain.

Doug wasn't a particularly intimidating guy or anything, but it just so happens that six months before that warm November afternoon, I'd actually placed an order for an even larger machine — a full size tractor. Now, you're probably thinking, *what?*

I don't know man. I was just moving to this house out in the country with 20 acres of woods and the previous owner had a tractor, our neighbor had a tractor, so... I just figured I needed a giant tractor too. But after a bit more learning about our property, I quickly realized I could get by with something much less beastly than that.

So I canceled my order for the tractor and placed another order with Doug for a ride on mower. Then, I decided to get an electric ride on mower instead from another company and canceled my order with Doug. I told him I needed a utility vehicle instead, which happened to be the fine utility vehicle that I was sitting in at the moment, six months later, having waited for this thing to get produced and arrive.

Months ago, when I had placed my order for the utility vehicle, Doug had given me a bit of a talking to. He said I changed my mind a lot. "Are you sure you want this machine before I place this order? It's a $500 non-refundable deposit," Doug said, looking at me sternly.

"Yes, I am sure," I told him.

So there I was, sitting in this damn thing, feeling anything but sure, but playing the part because... well... I didn't want Doug to be mad at me. Pretty crazy, huh?

But that's how niceness works.

We all want it to be different. We want to speak up, say no, create boundaries and make changes in our life, thus cementing a new and permanent way of being, leaving niceness behind forever. Then it's time to kick back as you coast through a life of freedom and ease. Right?

Well, maybe...

From what I've seen from clients and my own experience, it doesn't quite work like that. Instead of being a onetime wizbango transformation forever-more, it seems to be more of an ongoing process.

I would say there is a significant change of perception from "too nice" to "not nice." Once you've really gotten how to be more real and started practicing it regularly, it's hard to go back to life fully in the cage. Because deep within the cage of niceness, you are not only being good and nice, you also are convinced that it's good to be good and nice.

Once you've broken out of the cage and upgraded your mindset, you now see things differently. You become committed to authenticity rather than conformity and avoiding disapproval.

And yet, those patterns of people pleasing, avoiding conflict, and otherwise morphing yourself to be what others want are strong. They will tend to keep creeping up in different areas, again and again.

While you might initially think this is bad news, binding you to a life of perpetual niceness and limitation, nothing could be further from the truth. Instead, you can view each new reoccurrence of people pleasing or conflict avoidance as an opportunity. Life is the gym, and that urge to avoid and fawn is your fifty-pound weight — it's your strength training; it's your chance today to get stronger, become more, and gain even more freedom.

Because each time you see that niceness creeping in, you have a choice. And if you keep choosing realness, the level of authenticity and meaningful expression that you can expand to is limitless.

Furthermore, you get better at communication, leadership, and being a powerful force on this planet. You can achieve more, get better responses, create better relationships, and live a more authentic life on your terms.

So instead of being frustrated when you catch yourself being too nice, get curious. Choose compassion and humbleness over impatience, entitlement, and self-attack. That latter crew is much less fun to hang out with anyway. Compassion and humbleness are way better friends to spend your time with.

When you catch the pattern unfold, you can ask yourself: *Ahh yes, there I was, being nice again. I wonder what I was afraid of there?*

Do you see how simple it can be? How gentle? And at the same time, how growthful and honest and direct? We learn so much faster and better when we save our energy for learning and new action rather than wasting it away on self-attack, hopelessness, and self-pity.

To finish the work vehicle saga, I actually ended up taking that utility vehicle home even though it didn't feel right in my gut. I overrode my own intuition and inner knowledge to avoid the disapproval of a man I barely knew and would likely never see again.

When I got home, I drove that thing for one day around our land and instantly saw what I had done. I didn't want this thing. I had been too nice!

But instead of attacking myself, making it mean some horrible thing, or creating drama about it, I got curious. I was actually amused at the idea of doing something so extreme to avoid a stranger's disapproval. And most importantly, when I see niceness that doesn't serve me in my life, I instantly choose to act authentically and boldly.

So I phoned Doug and told him I didn't want it. There happened to be an electric version of the vehicle that wouldn't have all the exhaust smell, and I told him I wanted to return his one and put an order in for that one. At this point, I'm sure I was Doug's favorite (almost) customer.

But wait, it gets worse. Or perhaps, just more absurd. Now, I'm in the queue for an electric utility vehicle which will take another six months. While I'm waiting, one of our neighbors lets me ride his ATV. Whoah! Why hadn't I been aware of this? This thing was light, nimble, ultra-fast, great on the trails around our land, and could carry stuff and even haul a cart?

That's it! I went out and got one the very next day. We have it to this day, and it's absolutely awesome. And guess what? I had one more email to send. To Doug. Sweet Jesus.

But at this point, I was amused at the entire situation. I no longer needed Doug to like me. Heck, he probably thought I was bonkers. Or maybe that I was just an ignorant city dweller who was bumbling his way into country life. Which is actually pretty accurate.

So I sent an email requesting a cancellation of the electric utility vehicle. And, in the spirit of the last chapter of asking unapologetically, I even asked for my non-refundable deposit back! How dare I? Outrageous, I know. But the opposite of nice is freedom, my friend, so we're free to ask regardless of what the answer might be. Below is the email so you can see an example of asking unapologetically. In fact, my email isn't full of self-reproach, guilt, and excessive apology at all:

Hey Doug,

I decided to get an ATV for our property. I was able to use a neighbor's recently and I realized it fits our trails and needs better, as it's smaller and more nimble.

As a result, I'll withdraw my request for the electric gator. I understand I put a $500 deposit on it. If it's possible to get it back that would be ideal for our family (I imagine an electric gator will be quite easy to sell!)

If not, and the deposit must be forfeit, I understand.

Wishing you all the best during the holidays.

Aziz.

(In case you're wondering, the answer was "yes" and I got my money back, too).

CHAPTER 34

THE WINDING ROAD TO AUTHENTICITY

You being fully yourself, living the life you're meant to live is not a singular event. It's not a destination you reach then you set up camp and spend the remainder of your life resting in. Rather, authenticity is a moving target. It's the next aspect of you and your life path that you discover by being courageously curious and willing to take risks, fail, and learn through testing.

When you're living deep within the cage of niceness, you don't really know what you like or dislike, your true desires, what gives you meaning and purpose, or even how you truly want to express yourself around others. In essence, you don't really know yourself.

You've been hustling hard to play certain roles as well as you can so that others will approve, be impressed, or — at the very least — not dislike you. Instead of being curious about who you truly are, what makes you tick, and all your passions, foibles, and unique quirks, you're more focused on making sure that you are good and do things "right."

Thus, if you discover that you have a passion for something, such as sports, art, a particular person, or creative expression, you'll quickly check to see if that's "allowed." You'll ask yourself if it's okay to like this thing, what others would think about your desire, and if you should be this way or not. If your interest lies outside the bounds of who you are supposed to be, I'm afraid it gets the ax. It's buried under stories of being too busy, not being good enough to pursue it, or downplaying your actual desires.

That is life in the cage.

Fortunately, you've busted out of that thing, right?

It's a good thing, too, because it's worse there than you realize. When living in the cage, not only are you disconnected from yourself and not pursuing the life you really want, but you also aren't able to tune in to any greater guidance or purpose beyond fulfilling the roles properly. What life wants of you, why you're here, and what your higher purpose or calling might be all can't make it to you in that cage. More on this particular point later. For now, just know that being in the cage is not where you want to be.

As you step out of that oppressive reality into the sunlight, it might be a bit disorienting at first. I've had many clients tell me that once they stopped playing the nice role, they didn't really even know who they were or how to behave. We all hunger for freedom, but when we get it, it's often a little spooky. *You mean I can be… anyone?*

I encourage clients in this stage to start experimenting. You don't have to know exactly what's right; rather, just start paying attention to your urges, impulses, and subtle desires. Do you feel brighter, lighter, or more energized if you imagine doing something or spending time with someone? Move towards that. Do you feel heavy, tight, or repulsed when you imagine someone? Maybe that's a signal to move away.

Or, in the poetic words of Mary Oliver, "Let the soft animal of your body want what it wants."

This sounds beautiful and may even awaken something in your heart as you read it. And yet, for most of your life, you probably have not done this. Rather, you've carried on the nice conditioning, which isn't about being truly curious about the being you actually are. It's about molding and sculpting that being into whatever values and ideas are deemed "best" by the culture around you.

The classic example here would be the parents who want their children to excel in sports and academics so they perform well on the field and get into the best schools. The child might gravitate toward music, poetry, or art. This is all well and good when they're three. How cute. But when they're seven, and they'd rather draw than go to practice, that's no longer cute or acceptable.

I'm not saying those parents are bad. Perhaps that override sets that child up for a successful life that will present them with more money, more opportunities, and better health than if they grew up without it. But I'm not talking about then —I'm talking about now.

Now, you're an adult and are no longer being groomed and conditioned by your parents. Now, you are the one who's steering the ship and making the decisions for your life.

What if you became truly curious about who you actually are, rather than who you're supposed to be? At first, this is a scary prospect for clients. *But what I discover might be unacceptable, lazy, unworthy, unlovable, or bad. What if I discover* *that I'd rather spend time in the mountains than at my desk? I have a mortgage and a family and bills to pay! That's unacceptable.*

Easy tiger. I'm not saying be impulsive, quit your job, and move to the Rockies (although that might be a pretty cool adventure.)

Instead, what I'm saying is this: start to listen to yourself. What does that part of you hunger for? It longs for the mountains. Why? What's there? What do you feel when you're in the mountains?

My seven-year-old son is currently relentlessly determined to get a puppy. We already have two dogs in your family, but he wants a third. A small one. A toy poodle that he can cuddle. My wife and I are not anywhere near sold on this idea, as we've already raised two dogs, and a third seems like a lot.

But I'm curious about his experience. Why does he want a puppy? What about that puppy is different from our other dogs? What is he really hungering for?

When you do this with yourself, two amazing things happen.

First, just the act of listening makes a huge difference. For those who say "why spend the time daydreaming when the real world is waiting to punch you in the mouth?" they've most likely never actually slowed down and opened their hearts to themselves to listen with curiosity and compassion. They've dealt with their disappointment and resignation by putting a thick layer of tough guy/girl armor on.

Deep down, they have a dreamer inside too; it's just under a bunch of blankets, locked in the downstairs closet.

Instead of dismissing it, I suggest trying it. You'll discover the sweet and nourishing healing that comes from listening with curiosity. It conveys a message that you may have never really gotten as a child: *you matter; and what you feel and want matters.*

As you open and listen, the second amazing thing will happen: magic returns to your life. Most kids view the world with an aura of mysticism and magic. Anything can happen. Wonder and delight are everywhere.

When my second son was born and my wife was recovering from her C-section, my older son and I had a bunch of time to kill in the hospital. One activity he loved to do was wander up and down the halls and open up the cabinets and drawers that were built into the walls. Each time we'd get to a new drawer, he'd look back at me with wonder and delight in his eyes that said, *I wonder what's going to be in this one!*

In his little two-year-old mind, it seemed like it might have blankets, medical supplies, or… a purple unicorn! One cabinet didn't close right. When he closed it, it sagged down the side in a pathetic fashion. He looked back at me, pointed at the sagging door and laughed his head off.

Somewhere along the way, we get older, more hardened, and close our hearts to that delight, wonder and magic. Get real. Get a job. Get your head out of the clouds and see the world for what it is, just a bunch of stuff you have to do each day.

Never mind that we're experiencing all this through an inexplicable consciousness that is mysteriously alive, on a planet that is mysteriously alive in a cosmos that is, well, a complete and total mystery.

When you start to listen to yourself, feeling all the parts of you, all the yearnings and passions, you begin to plug back into this mystery. Maybe, just maybe, you'll find a way to act on what you discover. It might be a dramatic and radical change in your life. Or it might just be taking Friday off of work and spending the day out in the mountains.

The more you do this, the more you'll feel alive, connected to that great mystery that is pulsing just beneath the surface layer of our "ordinary" lives. You also might start taking more risks, asking spontaneously, and being open to the opportunities that continually arise in life.

In a relatively short span of time, you just might find yourself in a new place, with new people, doing something you'd never thought you'd be doing and feeling more delighted and alive than ever before.

CHAPTER 35

AUTHENTICITY...
IF IT'S ALLOWED

M ost clients I work with reach this crossroad once they've busted out of the nice cage. They've taken more bold action, challenged their inner safety police, and proven that all the stories in their heads are actually not true. They've gotten different responses then they predicted, positive responses, wins. Success! Yes, and... there's more.

Yes, they've escaped the cell, but in many ways, they're like fugitives on the run. Despite the bold actions and growth, the right set of challenging circumstances could plop them right back in the center of that cage, with the key nowhere in sight.

Can you relate to this? You take bold action, increase the amount of risks you're taking, and feel the confidence starting to build inside of you... but then something bad happens, or maybe just comfort seeking kicks in and you settle back into old habits, again.

What's happening here? Why is this so common?

This short-term liberation occurs because you have not fully claimed authenticity. Bold Authenticity. Living your life, fully. Instead, you've chosen authenticity if it's allowed, or what I would call Timid Authenticity.

Timid Authenticity means you are going to choose to be fully yourself... If others like it. Which means you are seeking to be fully yourself AND sustain the approval of the people around you. You're trying to be true to yourself, and still get accepted into that special club. You still think you need to please your parents, bosses, teachers, or that successful mentor, which will win you ultimate approval and acceptance, thus making you a "somebody."

This means you're still at odds with yourself; you're still not fully accepting and celebrating who you really are; you're still trying to play the roles in just the right way to finally prove that you're enough.

I'm not saying you don't want to succeed or that you shouldn't want your parents to be proud of you, or you shouldn't achieve notoriety in some sort of academic or business circles. What I'm saying is that if your top priority isn't authenticity, when push comes to shove, will throw that sucker in the back seat.

What you fail to realize is that by prioritizing authenticity, you can actually become more successful, free, and happier than ever before. Because when you fully own and celebrate who you actually are, you unleash your strengths and gifts at an entirely different level. Your hunger and drive switch from proving you're a somebody to fully living your life as just another human on this planet. Ironically, this humility, combined with courageous authenticity, bold action, and giving your gifts at the highest level often wins you all the opportunities of love and career success you so desperately strove for through your approval quest.

To put it simply, you can't have both. You can't boldly be yourself and live this life on your terms AND win everyone's approval. Heck, you can't win everyone's approval no matter how you live, but you can certainly dodge many of the direct attacks by flying under the radar and playing the good boy/ good girl role as best as you can. But when you step into authenticity, claim that as top priority, and start showing up fully in your life, that boat is for certain going to rock.

Family members might push back, your parents might shake their heads or cry, and your broader family or religious community might click their tongues. Strangely enough, there's no rhyme or reason to it, no right or wrong, as much as it seems that way. Let me give you a few examples from actual clients over the years to show you what I mean:

Samir's parents were disappointed with him for choosing to move to a different country and pursue online freelancing instead of staying put and becoming a doctor or engineer.

Rory's friends from high school and even some family members judged him for being too successful. He had chosen a career path in finance and made decisions to optimize his earning potential over the years. Family and old friends would make cutting comments about his house, his lifestyle, and how "it must be nice to have so much money to just waste it on all these unnecessary things."

Evan's father was chronically disappointed that his son was "just a nurse." Evan's father was a highly successful surgeon and regularly expressed concern about Evan's choices and the impoverished future he would have.

So… should you earn more or less? Devote more time to career and get ahead? Or does that make you too money-focused, greedy, and bad? I don't know; what did your conditioning tell you? Here's a few more examples outside of career and money:

Arjan grew up as a Sikh and had never cut his hair, as is one of the religion's obligations. When he was twenty-six he decided to cut his hair — his parents were devastated.

Amanda was a beautiful young woman, blossoming in her confidence and sexuality. She wore form-fitting clothes that showed off her fit figure, attracting attention of both men and women. She regularly received negative comments from her mother for "looking like a whore" and would sometimes get remarks from other women judging her for how she chose to dress.

Farah grew up wearing a hijab, a scarf that covers her hair and chest. This is a common type of clothing for many muslim women throughout the world. When she was young she was often mocked behind her back for wearing one, as she went to predominantly white, secular schools. When she was in her twenties, she decided she didn't want to wear it. Her family, especially her parents, were mortified and thought she'd lost it. In her thirties, once she had a family and several young children, she decided she wanted to start wearing a hijab again. Some of her friends questioned her for doing this, asking her "Why do you want to wear something that was obviously repressive and disrespectful to women?"

So... should Arjan keep all his hair? Should Amanda stop wearing those sexy clothes? Should Farah wear something over her hair, or not? That last one is especially confusing — is the hijab good or bad? What does it mean? Are her friends right?

I don't know what it means, but I know one thing for certain: every single one of these clients, and you as well, are screwed if you keep looking to the opinion of others to determine your life choices, both big and small.

That's a bottomless pit of confusing and mixed messages. Listening to those and acting on them will only take you further and further from yourself. What do I think Farah should do? She should wear whatever the hell she wants. Same goes for Amanda. Arjan can wear his hair in whatever way inspires and energizes him. For all those clients pursuing their careers, it's a very personal choice based on their desires, values, and unique strengths.

No one is going to give you authenticity. The demands on how you should be are not going to stop. Being angry and pouty that your parents have preferences about your life is not going to change anything. If you hate them, but then reluctantly do what they want — whoever the "they" is — then you are giving them authority over your own life and in many respects are choosing to live as a child.

Many parents, families, and cultures have a very clear idea of what roles are meant to be played. Their child is going to follow roles and they are going to do their part to ensure their kids are baked in just the right way to produce the muffin that fits right into the muffin tin mold.

Most people spend most of their lives sitting in the muffin shape, lamenting their dissatisfaction, and blaming others for the restrictions on them, all the while forgetting that they can choose, at any second of their lives, to completely break the mold and become whoever they want to be.

Authenticity is freedom, and if there's one thing that is an observable fact throughout human history it's that we need to fight for our freedoms. In any epoch, there's always a steady pressure for power to accumulate and oppress. Warlords, monarchs, and now the powerful institutions of today, all have a gravitational pull towards power accumulation at the expense of the rights of the average person.

Whether it's the right to eat at a restaurant regardless of your skin color, to work as a woman, to love who you love, or choose what medicines and chemicals go into your body, every single freedom you have was fought for by somebody at some point in time.

The same goes for your own authenticity right here and now. You, my friend, have to fight for it. If you're waiting for permission, waiting for someone to grant you authenticity and acceptance from everyone, waiting for a time when it's easy and comfortable and everyone around you celebrates your rebellious steps that challenge their worldview and sense of certainty... well, you'll be waiting for a long time.

CHAPTER 36

ROLES REVISITED

I want to show you something that might help you see the cage you were in and just how restrictive it is. Sometimes a simple image can change your perspective, which changes your choices, which changes your life.

Way back in Part I of this book, when you were a pleasing, nice, non-threatening friendly guy or gal, and not the savage beast that you have become today, do you remember learning about roles?

Essentially, roles are the little boxes that we put ourselves in to fit in, be liked, and survive. Here's a simple little image that will help you understand roles even more clearly, which is absolutely essential to living an authentic life.

Because your roles are confining you, often without you even knowing it. In fact, most people don't even know they're living within these roles and don't even see the millions of options they've cut off for themselves. Let me show you this graphic, and then it will become even more clear.

Above is a representation of all the different ways you could be a human animal on this planet. Each line, arrow, curve, or squiggle represents one possibility. You could dress one way, or another way, or another way. You could say virtually anything. You can have a million different beliefs, opinions, and perspectives. You can move your face and eyes and lips in thousands of different combinations. Heck, you could show up to work during the summer wearing purple rain boots, underwear on the outside of your pants, and a superhero cape. When someone asked you to provide your numbers for the weekly sales meeting, you could loudly proclaim, "I'm a one-eyed, one-eared, one-horned, flying, purple, people-eater!"

Instead of walking, you could hop. You could flip all your sentences so you spoke the words backward, one at a time. If you were in a conversation you didn't want to be in, you could simply turn around and walk away without saying anything, leaving that person mid-sentence.

I'm not saying you should (or would want to) do any of these things. Especially the purple people-eater line at work. That might cause some problems in your employment situation. But do you see how you, as a human animal, can do all of these things, and millions more?

This is represented in all these squiggly lines. The infinite possibilities of expressions, actions, decisions, and life paths you can choose.

Out of this infinite sea of possibilities, we choose to collapse it down into a very narrow set of prescribed perceptions and behaviors that fit a certain role. Let's take the Nice Person role as an example. This role has a small amount of the things you could do contained within it, and the rest is off-limits.

Inside this role, you can smile and nod when someone is talking, be attentive and interested, and ask questions to keep them talking. Not all questions, mind you. Only some questions. Polite questions. Questions that are not too edgy, nosy, or bothersome, or ones that would direct the conversations differently than where the other person wants to go (as if all people have agendas for conversations that they need to stay on).

Asking for what you want directly and saying no are probably outside the role of a nice person, at least most of the time. Perhaps if the situation got bad enough, then maybe you could put yourself first and ask for what you needed. Ending a conversation prematurely, telling someone you don't want to spend time with them, leaving a relationship or a job, or — gasp — giving someone critical feedback or even letting them go or firing them? You monster! How could you?

Since being disapproved of is generally undesirable to the nice person, then any thought, feeling, or behavior that someone might judge is also off limits. This shrinks that box down really tight into a small, confined, ultra-restricted way of life. That is why I call it "The cage of niceness."

Make no mistake, just because it's invisible doesn't mean it's not real and doesn't have the same confining effects as a physical cage.

To break free from this cage and live an authentic life where you are truly yourself and becoming who you're meant to be requires you to step beyond the confines of the Nice Person role, and any other role for that matter.

To be clear, all roles are not bad or something you should never engage in. Actually, we are playing roles all the time, and they serve a useful function. I play the role of dad with my kids. They need a dad, and they need me to be their dad. As the dad role, I will, on purpose, confine the infinite range of possibilities of what I could say and do around my kids to a more restricted range on purpose. The same goes for the roles you play at work, or on a date.

The problem is not the roles themselves; it's a compulsive need to play a role indefinitely, even though it might be extremely restrictive and confining. Sometimes you need to update a particular role to give you more space and freedom or to make it more effective.

As the role of dad, I limited myself too much when my kids were very young. I wanted to be a "good dad" which, as I had defined the role, involved not getting angry or raising my voice. Obviously, I wasn't able to completely adhere to that role because what parent throughout all of history never got angry or raised their voice? But nonetheless, I tried my best to keep living this way for years.

As you read that, you might think, *what's wrong with that role? That sounds pretty good to me.* While containing anger and treating my kids with care and respect are values I still hold to this day, I realized as they got older that sometimes they did need a dad who showed firmness in the form of strong energy, a raised voice, and a stern look. By the time they were five and seven, without that firmness, they had become wild beasts, defiant to all authority.

Hence, I need to expand and update my role of dad to include doing things that my dad used to do. Like getting upset and raising his voice. As much as I judged it while in my twenties, now that I'm forty, I have to be honest; that stuff works. They're running all over their mother, defying her very reasonable rules about not jumping off something or damaging the house, and then dad comes in with a stern look, a booming voice, and a command to "get off that right now!"...and they do it!

It takes humbleness to honestly look at the roles we're playing and consciously update and change them. The sense of pride and superiority I get from being "better" than my dad melted away as I humbled myself to grow and expand.

What roles are you playing? How are they working? Do you want to update or change any of them? If so, how?

As far as the "nice person" or "good person" role... that one might need a major overhaul. Man, if you knew what I used to think I had to be like in order to be a "good person"... the list was endless. Do everything for everyone, always be productive, never get upset, always be happy, always make others happy, never disappoint anyone, never make mistakes or fail, and on and on.

And sometimes, if you have a role that is so messed up, so bloated with old rules and conflicting demands, the best thing to do might just be to throw that sucker in the trash. Like a totaled car that would take just too much to repair, the best thing to do is to take it straight to the dump.

I actually encourage my very nice clients to stop trying to be a "good person." Because I know that role is absolutely too loaded. It's an utter minefield and most likely impossible to live up to. And it's certainly not pointing you towards authentically living your own life.

But...who would I be if I wasn't constantly pressuring myself to be a "good person?"

That's a great question. Let's find out.

CHAPTER 37

FIVE PERMISSIONS IN THE PURSUIT OF AUTHENTICITY

The tricky thing about discovering the "real you" is that it's not as simple or clear as buying a product online. You can't just scan through options, read some reviews, and then decide who you are. Instead, discovering and becoming your most authentic, true self is more similar to a treasure hunt. Better yet, for my fellow nerd friends, it's like a quest in which you must venture to unknown territory, face challenging situations, and find a variety of treasures, each one contributing to the overall quest. Then you take those items to Deckard Cain in the town of Tristam and... okay, I'll stop.

To put it simply, you might not actually know who you are or who you're meant to be. None of us do. Instead, you must discover who you are through learning, modeling, action, feedback, and guidance. It's an ongoing process, and the target is always moving because you are not fixed. You're always growing into the next version of yourself. Yet, the more you discover, the better you get to know yourself, and the better your life becomes.

I personally believe that who you truly are is guided by two primary factors. The first factor comes from within you. It's created by your personal interests, passions, and values. It's you steering your life in the way you want towards the things that are most meaningful to you. These things may differ from what is deemed meaningful in your family and culture, or what you were taught were the "good" or "right" things to pursue.

Most people are aware of this factor, and when they begin to pursue a more confident life on their terms, they focus heavily on it, which is typically very beneficial. However, if you only look within to find yourself, as determined by your personal interests and passions, ultimately, you'll still be missing something.

The second factor that determines who you are doesn't come from you. It comes from life around you. Where do you fit into the broader context, humanity, and the cosmos? What is life asking of you? What is the invisible hand of fate guiding you towards?

In essence, the call to become more of who you are is coming from within and without. In order to hear these calls and then have the ability to quickly and consistently heed the call, we must give ourselves permission. In fact, there are five key permissions you must grant yourself if you ever want to have a hope of radically increasing your sense of authenticity.

1. Permission To Discover

Surprisingly, most people never even give themselves permission to discover who they really are and who they want to be. The gravitational pull of the cultural field is too strong, and the fear of challenging this invisible force field is too great.

The whispers of destiny are often entirely ignored, drowned out by the much louder demands of the nice police commanding you to be who you should be to not upset or disappoint anyone. If you do challenge these inner dictates and actually begin to inquire into what you really want, what feels meaningful or important to you, etc., it's often done without much curiosity or passion.

Instead of an earnest curiosity to get to know yourself, it short-circuits the discovery process whenever you start to see something that is not how you "should" be. When big questions arise about your work, relationships, hobbies, and your entire way of operating in the world, you quickly shut the process down. *Why would I want to make a change in my relationship? That's bad and wrong!*

In order to discover who you really are, you must give yourself permission to discover who you really are! I know it sounds obvious, but watch what happens when you start to ask yourself with a true curiosity to see, hear, and know the real you as you are in this moment. Watch how much judgment arises. How much are you trying to alter, distort, or outright deny the answers that come back to you?

Instead of listening to these judgments and recoiling from the edge of the unknown lands, put on your leather armor and skull cap, embark on your quest, and get out into that spooky forest. It's the only way.

2. Permission To Be Wrong

The next challenge that prevents many people from discovering more about who they truly are is the fear of choosing the wrong things or simply being wrong. *How utterly terrible to be wrong. It stains the soul, you know. Shameful.*

As silly as it seems, that can stop someone from fully living their life, creating a tremendous amount of suffering for decades only to peak in a crescendo of regret in the final months before they die. Depressing, isn't it? Do you know someone like that? Perhaps someone very close to you?

The fastest way to discover what makes you tick, what you like and don't like, and what's most meaningful for you requires you to test many things out quickly.

I've met many clients who have been on the fence, pondering something for years before they met me. Should I move to a new state or not? Change jobs or careers? End this relationship? Start that business? Accept a leadership position?

They weren't sure if that was what they wanted or not, so they hesitated, delayed, and put their life on hold. First, for weeks, then months, then years. Then their desires became "someday, maybe" dreams, which, as we all know, tend not to happen because there is no "someday" on the calendar.

One of the first things I do to help these clients make the right decisions is to give them permission to make the wrong decisions. In fact, I encourage them to make decisions to discover rapidly what is right and what is wrong.

I also help them see that "wrong" is not a dirty word or a shameful failure. "Wrong" is actually extremely valuable data because it shows you a path that is not what you want to go down in your life. If you're at a fork in the road, trying to see which path to go down by craning your neck to try and see over the bushes, you'll spend your whole life hesitating. You don't have enough data to reach a meaningful conclusion. Therefore, you need to walk down a path for ways and see what information you receive from that action.

One of my clients was a physician who worked in a hospital and taught residents. He had considered for over five years if he should start a private practice. But what if he didn't like it? What if it felt overwhelming? What if it was the wrong move?

Within two months of starting our work together, he began the process of setting up a private practice. He got the appropriate permissions from his hospital employer, found an office, got a biller, and took many other necessary steps to make this vision a reality. He then put the word out to colleagues and online and, within another month, had several new patients. Success! Except that his worst fears were realized — he actually didn't like it! Terrible, right? I know. I made sure to chastise him heavily in our sessions, chanting "shame" and going on and on about staining his soul. No, I'm kidding.

In reality, we celebrated the "wrong" move and helped him extract the learning from the experience. He got to know himself better, including what he likes and values, and finds most fulfilling in his work life. Now, in the future, he can make better decisions faster because he has real, up-to-date, accurate information about himself.

Therefore, if you want to feel more decisive, get to know yourself faster, and take control of your life, it's time to start being wrong.

3. Permission To Make Mistakes

This one may sound pretty similar to Permission #2, and "mistake" might seem like another word for "wrong," but it's quite different. Let me illustrate why with a client's story.

Just the other night, on a mastermind call, a woman who we'll call Ruby was sharing her concerns about creating relationships, especially romantic relationships. She was deathly afraid of coming across as needy, which, in her mind, was horribly repulsive. She described how her friends had given her advice about playing hard to get and not showing much interest upfront with men she dated. That would ensure she didn't come across as needy, thus repelling them and destining her for a lonely single existence forever and ever.

She recently had gone on several dates with a man and was in agony over whether she was sharing too much, appearing too needy, and generally worrying about how she was coming across.

Initially, we focused on helping her calm her tense nervous system, sending a message to herself that someone judging her was not a serious threat to her existence. As she began to calm down, I realized of all the things I could help her with, Permission #3 would provide the most immediate benefit.

I shared how there are patterns in dating and interpersonal relationships that tend to work better than others. For example, asking for what you want tends to work better than screaming and demanding it or being totally silent and hoping they'll read your mind. Being able to feel infatuated with someone and contain it, rather than telling them on your second date that they're "the one" and asking them, "What should we name our kids?" is generally more likely to keep that new relationship going.

Of course, trying to hide all interest and enthusiasm and play it super cool doesn't really work that well, either. It can feel false and forced, and it can lead to you stifling beautiful things that could actually deepen the new bond and create exciting and passionate love for you both.

Basically, you have to learn through doing. Sometimes maybe you overshare. Other times you under share and hold back too much. Sometimes you share openly, and the other person seems to not like it, and you think you shared too much. But then you realize that you actually shared a healthy amount, and that person has some blocks or fears about being real. Confusing, huh? Relationships are never clear-cut with black and white lines. It's a murky world of feelings, beliefs, and value systems.

How do you want to be with a new partner? Do you value openness and honesty? Do you like relationships where you can share more authentically? I sure do. In fact, that became a requirement for me in my dating life and something I actually tested for quite early. I would ask more direct questions and share more openly about what I was noticing and experiencing at the moment.

One woman I dated who liked to party and drink with her friends as her primary hobby told me, "You've studied too much psychology." In other words, "I don't like that and stop being that way." But instead of imploding with shame, as I would have certainly done in the past, I saw that we weren't a good fit. My drinking days were done, and I was looking for depth.

Less than one year later, I met Candace, and our experience of sharing and being real with each other was very different. Rather than her shutting down authentic sharing, she encouraged and strengthened my ability to be this way.

So how do you know right now at this moment, with this person, as you're fretting over whether they're going to text you back or not — *should I have shared that? Am I coming across as too excited? Too needy??*

You, my friend, need much more permission to make mistakes. Sometimes you might come across as too needy. And that's okay. Can you see how much intense judgment and shame there is around this? How little permission do you give yourself?

Take a full breath in, and on the exhale, allow your belly to soften. Repeat this, and on the next exhale, soften both your belly and your jaw. Repeat this a few more times, each time relaxing the pressure while intentionally giving yourself permission to learn through practice.

You're allowed to make mistakes in dating, relationships, speaking up at work, with clients and colleagues, on projects, in your hobbies, and even with your bigger life decisions. The more you can separate yourself from the intense shame and self-judgment, the more you can compassionately navigate the confusing and often challenging waters of close relationships and career struggles.

4. Permission To Be Messy

I don't know about you, but I sure like cleanliness and order. Spending the last decade raising two young, wild boys has definitely been a challenge to the part of me that likes everything to be in its place.

The two creative forces of the universe — order and chaos — definitely play out in our household. I, obviously, am championing the righteous cause of order. In the rooms that I have the most control over, such as my office or the garage, there is a place for everything. Systems are optimized, then optimized again. It's clean. And boy is it satisfying.

The boys' bedrooms and the family room, on the other hand, are breeding grounds of creativity, high-energy fun, and utter chaos. Sometimes I make a valiant foray into those lands of havoc, hacking back piles of toys, plastic bits, and other essentials that my kids insist we can't possibly get rid of. But soon, I am overwhelmed at the prospect of organizing such disarray, and I retreat back to the safety of the other rooms of the house.

As much as I do appreciate order and cleanliness in the physical world, I have come to learn that close relationships are anything but. I used to try to keep my close relationships clean and orderly as well. I didn't want to make any messes, any ruptures, any chaos.

You know, the classic nice person patterns. I don't want to upset others, make waves, damage relationships, upset or burden people. I want everyone to get along and everything to be nice and clean.

Anger is messy. Saying something that I'm not 100% certain I mean is messy. Figuring out what I really think and feel through discussing it with another person is messy. Showing irritation, anxiety, sadness, or any other "negative" emotion is messy. Fights? Get out of here! Too messy.

The problem is relationships don't function like an optimized pantry. In the latter situation, it's efficient and awesome. But when you keep out all the mess in your relations with others, you just end up keeping the real you out.

Then you're left playing the role that you think you're supposed to play, which absolutely hemorrhages your energy. Everything starts to seem boring, irritating and frustrating, or pointless. You seek energy in suboptimal ways, trying to power up from junk food, increased caffeine or sugar intake, or scour your phone apps, hoping some exciting new notification will give you some juice.

But you and I both know none of this really works. You don't need the pseudo-energy of outrage from a social media app. You need the life force energy that flows through all living things that you naturally feel when you are living closer to your source, your authentic self.

So from here forward, give yourself permission to be messy. Have the conversation before you're totally ready. Prep for a bit ahead of time if you'd like, then dive in, unsure of exactly how it will go and where it will lead you. Say what you really want with your friends, letting them know what you like, don't like, and everything in between. Let others really see and know you as you are in this moment. I know it's not all clean and orderly, but many people would say our family room is the funnest room in the entire house.

5. Permission To Change... Then Change Again!

There's a strange phenomenon in many cultures throughout the world today in which people view it as embarrassing or shameful to change. Politicians will proudly proclaim that they don't "flip-flop" and that they've stayed the same on a particular issue for twenty years.

I sure hope I don't think, perceive, feel, and believe the same things in twenty years. I hope my software has been updated twenty times over in those two decades. And if you are seeking to be more free to be you in this world, I'd encourage you to adopt this permission to grow and change as well.

A common concern among clients who attend my events or join my mastermind program can be summarized as, "But what if people see that I'm different all of a sudden?" as in, they've been quiet, reserved, or passive for many years, and if they were to suddenly show up more bold, expressive, outspoken, or assertive, then others would judge them negatively for changing.

The solution to this concern is to treat it as a non-issue and celebrate your ability to change. I often like to demonstrate how you might respond to that imaginary critic:

"Wow, you're so different all of a sudden. What's gotten into you?"

"Thanks for noticing! Yeah I just decided life's too short and I wanted to speak up more."

This is just one of a hundred ways you could respond. The point is you'll quickly notice that it's not hard to think of a response at all. The problem is you are afraid of the change. This is rooted in the old illusion that the real you is somehow not good enough for love and belonging, that there is something specific or vague that is totally off or "wrong" about you.

This illusion gives birth to the nice-person persona where you play by all the rules, try extra hard, minimize your needs so as to not burden or bother others, and just be a good boy or girl.

Authenticity is the opposite of this persona. The opposite of nice is you, and there's only one way to get there. You must challenge the illusion and test out your old stories again and again until they dissolve back into the shadows from which they formed.

Once you've granted yourself permission to change and then change again, life takes on a much more magical quality. Like a kid who decides he wants to be Superman one day and then an astronaut the next, you can let yourself rapidly explore and try on different dreams, desires, and expressions.

Several years ago, during the peak lockdown period of the pandemic, I began hiking more than I used to. I began exploring more of the trails near my home and eventually discovered Mt. Hood — one of the most extraordinary places I've ever seen. Over the next few years, I passionately hiked and ran all around Mt. Hood, Mt. Saint Helens, and The Sisters Mountains in Oregon. Running and hiking around mountains became my thing.

A year ago, we moved into our dream home in the woods. It has acres and acres of forest, a pond, and beautiful giant trees encircling an extraordinary, secluded house. Part of moving out to the country involved learning how to take care of everything out here, so I learned how to use and maintain machines such as chainsaws, wood-splitter, ATVs, and compact tractors. So now, using machines and taking care of the house and property is my thing.

Many years ago in college, I spent countless hours playing video games and learning the classical guitar. Those were my things. I don't really do either of those anymore.

I'm sure you can see for yourself how your hobbies, passions, and interests change over years and decades. But that's just the tip of the iceberg. So much more of you changes over time if you let yourself flow with that ever-moving river of authenticity.

Your beliefs, political perspectives, and perspectives about the world will change as you have more experiences, play different roles, and grow as the world around you changes and evolves rapidly. Who you're in a relationship with might change, and even how you relate changes as well. If you're developing your confidence and authenticity, then your capacity to give and receive love and let yourself be deeply seen and known expands as well.

I invite you to let go of any idea that you're supposed to stay with a particular perspective, passion, or way of being for your entire life. Change and evolution are not shameful or signs of weakness. They are the golden thread to follow to an extraordinary existence in which you feel more and more alive with each passing year.

CHAPTER 38

THE GENTLE CURRENT

Okay, I have some news for you that I've been waiting to tell you. I wasn't quite sure when the best time was, so I just decided to do it now. So here we go.

To be clear, I'm not a big fan of permanent labels or diagnoses. In fact, I've oriented my life towards liberation and going beyond the limits of the labels I've been given. Instead of "managing" my social anxiety, I became obsessed with liberating myself so now I can do things socially that most people would shy away from, such as leading groups, public speaking, and being intentionally very vulnerable in my public teaching and writing.

I spent several decades severely limited by chronic pain and an autoimmune disorder, and I continually pushed the edge, sensing there was a way out. Now I can run in the mountains for fifty miles, play tag with my kids, and enjoy the extraordinary gift of a healthy body.

And, having said all that, as much as I want to say that niceness is something that you can free yourself from forever,

I have to say there may be a bit of a pitfall there. Let me explain.

Niceness, conflict avoidance, and people-pleasing are actually quite sophisticated social patterns. They are not like social anxiety, which basically has you run and hide (aka avoid) the people and situations you're scared of. No, with niceness, you still talk to people, carry on conversations, do your job, and interact with your friends and dates or partner.

Unbeknownst to you, at any given moment, that urge to please, that tendency to hold back, that split-second decision to dodge the conflict, even just a little bit, can creep in and influence you. And very quickly too.

What I've found in my life is that there is an invisible energetic current gently pushing me towards niceness. Much like a gentle current in a river or ocean, you may not even see which way it's going. But make no mistake, it's persistently pushing you in a very specific direction.

At first, when you're in the water, you might not even notice it. You're just frolicking around in the waves, but when you look back at the shore, you've traveled several hundred yards.

Similarly, the gentle current of niceness creates invisible pressure for subtle nice behavior. Nothing crazy or over the top. But perhaps the persistent need to reassure people all the time and the fear of having anyone feel "bad" about themselves. This causes you to not speak directly or give clear feedback, even when it's needed.

You might have a barely perceptible compulsion to make your communication sound more enthusiastic or friendly, to smile more, to make your texts have lots of exclamation marks, and to treat others as if they are fragile and easily wounded by you.

You might go into a conversation having a clear sense of what you want, and what you're going to say "yes" to and "no" to, but by the end of the conversation, you've agreed to something you hadn't planned on or wanted to.

These examples are not general or hypothetical. They are exact patterns I've noticed in myself and many clients. And even though I've dedicated myself to studying this topic and done a ton of inner work and outer action to upgrade these patterns socially and in relationships, when I entered into the wide world of being a boss, I brought all those patterns with me.

As I began to grow my business as an author, teacher, and coach, I invested in business coaching and training programs. I learned about marketing, sales, and how to reach the people I wanted to help online. When my business coaches learned I was doing everything myself, the first thing they told me was that I needed help. I needed to hire somebody.

And so I did. I hired my very first part-time assistant. A sweet woman who truly wanted to help me and my business. But my oh my, her life was a mess. Five kids, dental issues, health issues, getting a puppy, getting married, getting divorced, and on it went. I hired her for 10 hours per week, and each week, she struggled to reach that number of hours.

"Well, Aziz," you might say. "No big deal. You just mishired. Simply let her go and find someone new. No problem."

Indeed that sounds like a reasonable thing to do. So I did... after two years. Yep, two years of eeking along, struggling for her to meet her hours, random sick days due to kid issues, and so much more.

I couldn't fire her. She needed my help. I mean, look at the state her life was in! Besides, when she did work, she got the job done pretty well, I guess. I had a hard time being direct, offering feedback, correcting her work, and basically anything else that involved being not nice.

At the same time, I was bold and expressive with clients in my romantic relationship and in my personal life. What gives?

I know it might sound crazy, but not only was I running all these nice guy patterns as a boss, but I also wasn't even that aware of it. That's the fascinating part about the gentle current... Sometimes it takes a long, long time before you really see it.

But eventually, I did, and I made the hard decision to let her go and look for something else. Clearly, then, I learned my lesson and would be making decisions boldly and in my best interest from then on, right? Not quite.

You see, at the root of niceness, there is a core misperception, an optical illusion that makes you see something incorrectly. This error in perception can be summed up as: *there's something not quite good enough about me. Not complete, or whole, or worthy. And so I need others to complete me because I'm not enough to succeed or thrive myself. Therefore I'll be sure to never upset them too much so they never leave me.*

Now, I realize that humans are interdependent social creatures, and we all do need others to survive. But that's not what I'm talking about. What I'm referring to is the mistaken belief that gets you into a relationship that isn't great for you, but you stay in because "I need this person or I'll die", or "they need me or they'll die."

This belief makes you latch onto others and sell yourself a delusion that without them, you'd never make it. Instead of the reality that if it doesn't work with this person, you can always find someone else, someone better for the job, or the relationship.

While I'd largely healed that story in my social life and romantic relationships, it was running rampant in business. I knew I was good at helping people. I had enough experience and evidence to have grounded confidence in that. But reaching people online, marketing, selling, and running a business? No, I wasn't good enough to do that, and so I needed people and latched onto them like a baby koala to its mother.

Eventually, I worked up the nerve to let my assistant go and hired two employees and a contracted sales team. Going bigtime. And all the while, the gentle current pushed me towards being nicer, and nicer, and nicer. But here's the key point I want you to see... it wasn't obvious. I did have boundaries with team members, I did say "no" to many things, I did have direct conversations.

In fact, many of the nice ways I behaved didn't seem like overly nice behaviors, they seemed good, or the "right" way to be. I wanted to be a good boss, so I started my team at good salaries. One of my team members had a health issue, so I got the best healthcare possible for my employees. That's the right thing to do, isn't it?

My sales team had suggestions for my marketing plans, so I implemented them as best I could. That's being open-minded and willing to grow, isn't it? In fact, they raved about me and complimented me on being so open to trying new things. I beamed with pride at being a "good client" of this sales team.

This level of subtle niceness might not sink your life or cause a train-wreck in your relationships. It's not terrible. It's just not optimal. Something is off...

I was paying my team members a lot. Were they the best for their jobs? Could I find something better for cheaper? Someone with more skills, a better attitude, or more varied skill sets? I don't know because I didn't ask. I also felt a background pressure to make sure they felt good, worthy, and valuable. I felt like I had to continually raise their salaries and say "yes" to raise requests, regardless of whether they had helped the company actually generate more income.

Was this sales team optimal? Were they the best at sales? Were they fully in integrity, and did they do sales the way I did? I don't know because — well, actually, I did ask. And they wouldn't tell me. In fact, I wanted them to record their sales calls so I could listen to them, and they refused, which, knowing what I know now about business, is a big red flag.

But I pushed a little, and then relented. Which is what you do when you're too nice. You ask, or push back, a little. But not too much. Remember, you don't want to upset people too much and drive them away.

I told myself, *I need these people, I need this team. I can't make it without them.* A strange form of selective amnesia, isn't it? Have you ever done that? Have you ever told yourself you can't live without this person, somehow forgetting the many decades of your life before you knew that person?

I'm not going to bore you with the nitty gritty details, but let's just say that over a period of years my business became less and less my own. I had arrangements in which I became overly dependent on various people — none of whom were bad or malicious — they just were looking out for what was best for them. And I believed that I needed them to survive, so I let the gentle current slowly contort me.

In your case at first, those contortions aren't so bad. Just move your arm a little this way, your foot a little what way; but month after month, year after year, all of a sudden you'll be all pretzeled up with your elbow dislocated and your head up your ass.

And so it goes… until it doesn't.

Because at any moment, you just might wake up, look at the shore, and see how far you've drifted from yourself. And if you've broken out of that niceness cage once before, you know you can do it again. Yes it's scary, and it feels like you might die. But you know that living in that cage, even if you were to survive, is no real life at all.

And so I began the controlled demolition. I systematically let go of team members over a six month period, cutting loose people and roles in the business that I had told myself for years would certainly sink the ship. It was scary as hell.

Some people took it well, with maturity and we concluded on good terms with the possibility of even working together in the future. Other people took it as a personal affront, a betrayal. Because they'd bought into the story that I needed them as well. How dare I leave? One of them even told me on the way out that I couldn't make it without him. Yes, I might hustle to survive, but I'd never thrive or succeed without him. Like Elvis and Colonel Tom Parker.

Now, in case you are going through, or have ever gone through one of these controlled demolitions in your life, that has involved ending things with a partner, changing things with a family member, letting people go, or leaving a job or company, let me tell you this. If, on the way out, the person is berating you, telling you that "you're nothing," that "nobody could ever love you," that "you'll never make it," do not listen to them!

Instead, listen to the message underneath, which is: *Thank God you're getting out!* That is not the kind of relationship you need in any aspect of your life.

So now, on the other side of all this, I have a word of caution for myself and my clients. Beware of that gentle current. Don't assume that you're no longer a "nice person" and you got all that handled once and for all.

Instead, I invite you to think of it as being in shape. Yes, you might be in great shape now, exercising regularly, getting good sleep, eating healthy foods in just the right amounts. You're crushing it. Strong. Capable.

And in order to keep that strength you must be self-aware and continually choose those same habits again and again. In order to preserve your strength of character, boundaries, assertiveness, and authenticity, you must repeatedly strengthen yourself by practicing those boundaries, saying no, having direct conversations, sometimes upsetting others, ending things that don't work for you, and on and on.

You must remind yourself before the very next assertive conversation, even if you've had thirty just like it before, that you have a right to say no, that conflict is not fatal, and that being direct now will save you months or years of pain. You must give yourself permission daily to be 100% unapologetically you. To be more direct and less nice. To leave out the exclamation marks in your messages, or the excessive thank you's or apologies.

You must paddle against that gentle current every day, or it will ever so slowly take you right back to nice person island. And you don't need me to tell you this, but trust me, that place sucks.

CHAPTER 39

BEING LIKED VS BEING KNOWN

"I want them to accept me and the choices I've made," he said.

"Of course," I replied. "It always feels better to be accepted than rejected…" I paused for a moment, then continued. "But what if they don't?"

He grimaced. Apparently that meant it was not good.

But really, what choice did he have? What choice do you have?

This particular client had made a choice four years ago to conclude his marriage and initiate a divorce. He had tried for years to make his marriage work, primarily for his three children, but after pushing for so long, he finally decided to stop and move in a new direction.

His children were upset. And then, several years later, when he got into a new romantic relationship, they were even more upset. One in particular — his oldest daughter —

was angry and didn't want to acknowledge her father's new partner or even speak with him.

Yes, it's painful, but what is there to do? He couldn't make his daughter accept him. Just like you can't make anyone like or love you. Sure you can hustle and try to win their favor, but at what cost? For them to truly admire, respect, accept, or love you...that must be freely given.

The question then is, what are you choosing to go for in your relationships and life. Are you going to pursue acceptance and the illusion that you can somehow win and sustain it? For this particular client, that would have meant staying in a dissatisfying marriage and letting his romantic and sexual life wither in order to maintain the approval of his children.

For you that might mean working somewhere, paying for something, giving something, or otherwise staying in a situation that doesn't work for you. You might feel the need to smile, agree, avoid saying what you really think, don't ask questions, and hold back in all your social interactions to try and eek out some semblance of approval.

Barf. Or...

You can make a new choice. Instead of striving for acceptance, you prioritize being deeply known by others, and in turn to know them. This means you take the risk to be who you really are and want to be, from the big life choices like who you marry, down to the smallest daily choices like how you dress or what you say at a dinner party.

When you choose being known, you let acceptance come, or not, as an effect of being who you are around others. In other words, you make the choice to be you and share who you are with the world, and allow others to react in whatever ways they will.

This doesn't necessarily make the moment when someone is rejecting you easy or comfortable. I wouldn't expect my client to feel carefree or delighted about his daughter's pain and upset. But it does change how you see the situation, and indeed your entire life. It helps you know what to do.

You find a sense of solidity and self-trust in your choices and how you're called to steer your life. Instead of someone's disapproval being a sign of alarm that you're doing something wrong, it simply shows you that they are making some meaning out of whatever it is you're doing or not doing, and they don't like it.

I encouraged my client to continue to reach out to his upset daughter. To tell her "I know you are upset with me and don't approve of some of the choices I've made in life. And that's okay. You can have mixed feelings or dislike things I've done. And, you are my daughter and I want to have a deep, lifelong relationship with you. You matter to me. I'd rather talk through our upsets rather than hold ice-cold grudges for years. To me that seems so sad, to imagine missing out on life together because we didn't want to have it out and simply hear our differences directly."

The question for you is, what have you been prioritizing thus far in your life — being liked or being known? How has that worked for you? Are you ready to make a change? To make a new choice to reclaim your power and focus on what you actually can control, rather than grasping for something elusive outside of yourself.

If you were focused on being known and knowing others, what might you do today? How would you show up at work, or with your family or friends?

CHAPTER 40

You Will Be Disliked

The other day I opened up audible to download yet another book. This one I'll listen to all the way through, I swear. As I found the book I was looking for, I scrolled through the reviews, curious what people were saying. The first review I came across had a blisteringly negative review of the narrator. This person said:

"As for the narration... I've listened to hundreds of books and this may be the worst narrator I've heard. His ostentatious, over-enunciation came across as smug, irritating, and highly artificial. It was enough to seriously distract from the content of the book."

Yikes. Sounds pretty bad, huh? As I scrolled further, something fascinating emerged. I saw other people not only loved the narrator, but titled their reviews things such as: "Bravo to the narrator!" or "Narrator is amazing!"

Go figure. What's happening here? Is the narration bad or good? The worst or the best? The answer is... yes. It depends on who's listening to it. Or, seeing it another way, the answer is neither. The narrator is neither good or bad, awesome or terrible. He just is. He reads in a certain style and some people love it, and apparently, some people find it smug and irritating.

There is absolutely nothing you can find in this universe — animal, plant, mineral, or thing, that someone out there doesn't love and someone else doesn't hate. Oh, and don't forget, the vast majority of people who'd fall somewhere in between, mostly in the indifferent or "don't know, don't care" category.

The mountains? I love them. Most forms of candy? Hate it. Running? Love it! Swimming? Meh, I guess I could learn to like it if I had to do it a lot. You have the exact same range of likes, dislikes, and in-betweens as me and everyone else, except what you love is different from me and others.

Even objectively "the best" people and things, such as the best player in a particular sport is not universally loved or even liked. So while you can objectively measure the fastest person or the best free throw shooter at a given time that says nothing about their likeability. In fact, because they're probably famous, that means more people know of them, and while they may have legions of fans who love them, they also have more people hating them than the total number of humans that will ever know of you or me. That's a lot of hate.

Many humans hate others who are particularly remarkable or excellent at something because they feel insignificant in comparison. This bitter brew of inferiority and insignificance leads to a puffing up through the pseudo superiority of judging that sports figure as "a jerk," or "sell-out," or some other label indicating that they're worse (and therefore the judger is better).

Are you a man or a woman? Lots of people out there dislike people in those categories. Are you nonbinary in your gender? Even more dislike there. If you fit into dominant cultural norms in your society, you might dodge some dislike, but certainly not all of it. People can dislike you because of your skin color, gender, location, country of origin, sexual orientation, accent, hairstyle, political preferences, beliefs, religion, or any one of a thousand life choices you make based on your values.

People close to you will have judgments about you for what you choose, how you live, and what you decide to do or not do. Someone could be upset because you left the milk out; someone could be disappointed because you said no to them; someone could dislike you because they feel jealous about something you're excelling at.

Whether it's your closest family, friends, and loved ones, or people from another city, state, or country who don't even know you, you will be disliked. Sometimes the dislike is temporary and fades quickly, as is often the case with those close to you. Sometimes, it's calcified in the minds of someone who's never met you, who is attempting to avoid their own pain through choosing judgment or hatred of someone they've never met. Regardless of who or where, one thing is for certain: you will be disliked.

Are you with me? Can you see the inevitability of this fact? Can we agree that there is no way you can be — no matter how agreeable and pleasing — that would appeal to every human on this planet and not garner some judgment or dislike? And so being disliked is inevitable. This is a hard fact of life, like death or taxes. They're just going to happen no matter what you do.

Given the setup, the way I see it there are two possible ways to take this hard truth. Option one is it's terrifying because you perceive someone's dislike as dangerous, and since dislike can come at you from anyone, anywhere, at any time, for any reason, your threat system is stuck in the ON position, firing 24/7 in danger mode.

This option is obviously terrible, so what's the alternative? What if the fact that you will be disliked is actually a huge relief?

What if you don't need to make an effort to avoid being disliked? What if dislike were an inevitable part of life and you expected that it would happen each day, week, month, and year? Hence, when dislike rears its ugly head, instead of an inner response of "oh no!" you think "of course!"

Of course someone got angry at me while I was driving because they wanted to go faster. Of course my friend got irritated with me when I showed up 20 minutes late to pick them. Of course that person dislikes me because I'm a _____ (man, woman, lesbian, feminist, vegan, meat-eater, black, Indian, rich, vaccinated, unvaccinated).

Think of yourself as having a dislike quota. I know, I know. It can be hard to swallow at first. I mean... me? People out there will dislike me?? But I'm so pleasant! Yes, I'm afraid so. So what if you have a dislike quota in which at any given time there's going to be one to three people that you know of who are upset in a relationship with you.

This doesn't have to mean they hate you and have unleashed a death wish curse upon thee. The level of upset might vary greatly in degree or even in which type of emotional upset they feel. As I write this, I may have one client who is angry at me for calling on someone else instead of him in a group call last night, my son might be sad because we didn't play enough games for his liking before I left for work in the morning, and my mom might feel a little hurt that I haven't responded to her text yet.

These are hypothetical of course. I'm not sure if any of these people are actually upset with me at the moment. Maybe it's an entirely different set of three. Or maybe it's just one at the moment. Or ten for all I know. Heck, as I reach more people through books, podcast episodes and interviews, YouTube videos, and other online avenues, right now there could be a hundred different people who are turning off a recording of me somewhere in irritation and disgusted dislike. *This guy! Harrumph! Terrible!*

What if you similarly have a quota of people who are currently disliking you, or could be at any time? And what if this were perfectly okay and nothing was wrong? No threat, no danger, no cause for panic and alarm. All is well.

If the person who is upset with me is someone I know personally, then I may interact with them about their upset. Either they will bring it up to me, or I may ask them proactively if they send me a snarky text or make a passive-aggressive comment. If, however, they work through their upset on their own without bringing me in at all, that's fine too. Many of your upset quota people will deal with their feelings without you ever knowing about it. Like wind howling through the mountains three hundred miles away.

Can you feel that emerging sense of relief? It's the kind of relief that comes when you stop fighting the weather. I've lived in the Pacific Northwest for over a decade, and if there's one thing this region is known for, it's rain. It typically rains late September through mid-June. That means on any given day during the fall or winter, and a lot of the spring, what's going to happen? That's right, rain!

I used to resist the rain. Not overtly with lots of complaining, but more subtly. I'd feel discouraged if I saw a 10 day forecast of rainy days. I'd dislike my running shoes getting wet and having to dry them. I'd secretly wish it were more sunny.

And then one day, I decided to completely surrender to the weather because other than moving I had absolutely no control. Once I made this decision, I saw that the discomfort when the rain came wasn't the rain's responsibility. It was mine. The discomfort is something that I need to face, overcome, and transform my relationship to.

I invite you to adopt the exact same stance towards dislike. Because like the rain in Oregon, it's going to come. We've already established that. So first, I suggest you stop trying to avoid it.

Have you ever seen someone out in the rain trying to avoid the rain? It's a pathetic site. They're scurrying around like an ant who's colony has been demolished by a boot. They hide their face in an attempt to escape the onslaught of wetness. They react as if the rain is somehow harming them.

They might even have a story that says "If I get wet, I'll get sick!" which is a nocebo effect that might even result in them generating an illness even though there's no physiological reason that wetness or cold will make you sick. In fact, research done on Wim Hoff, the Ice Man himself, has shown that regular cold exposure strengthens your cardiovascular system and can make your immune system much more effective at fighting off pathogens.

In much the same way, dislike is not dangerous. It can feel uncomfortable, like wet or cold rain. But it can't hurt you. Your beliefs about the upset, which you conclude means you're a "bad person" and are therefore unlovable, unworthy, or otherwise threatened in your ability to connect with others, create the turmoil.

It would be prudent for me to add one caveat to my statement that dislike is not dangerous. There are certain circumstances — such as an abusive relationship or people with intense hatred and an intent to harm — who may act out their dislike with violence. This is a very small fraction of the dislike pie, and hence in the vast majority of cases in your life, you can simply tolerate the dislike and know it's unpleasant yet not dangerous. Then there are those times when it's best to get the F out of dodge. Now. I'll leave that discernment up to you.

CHAPTER 41

THE LIBERATION TONIC:

HOW TO EMOTIONALLY HANDLE BEING DISLIKED

One thing I often hear from clients is that they intellectually get that not everyone will like them. As much as they know that with their heads, it seems like their hearts, or their entire nervous system, still reacts strongly when someone doesn't like them.

In fact, their internal pressure, tension, anxiety, or stress might even kick into high gear at just the possibility of someone disliking them. So how do we change this? How can you become truly more relaxed with someone judging you, being upset with you, or disliking you?

It appears there is a magical cocktail of several ingredients that, when mixed together, produces a powerful antidote to approval-addiction-itis. These magical ingredients are:

1. A true or deep acceptance of who you are at this moment in your life.

2. Permission to live by your rules (aka living *your* life, not someone else's)

3. Space for others to have their own perspectives and live in their own version of reality, that might differ from yours.

I'll break each one of these down to make it even more clear, plus provide a few techniques you can use to access these ingredients for your own magical cocktail. I think this mixture needs a catchy name don't you? How about **liberation tonic**.

To illustrate how to access and mix the three ingredients of this tonic, let me share a recent experience with a client in my year-long confidence-building mastermind program. Brian is a fit, intelligent, attractive man in his early thirties who lives with a number of housemates in New York City (because rent there is apparently a billion dollars per square foot).

Whenever he'd leave his room to go to the kitchen, eat in the dining room, or spend time in any common area, he'd feel a pressure to talk with others, be funny and engaging, and essentially entertain anyone and everyone. This isn't surprising as he received some fairly strong conditioning from his mother that taught him that he was responsible for her emotional state and that he had to be light and fun to "keep mom happy."

Flash forward twenty years, and now he feels he has to "keep everyone happy" by entertaining them. That makes making some dinner and eating it at the table sort of an ordeal. Especially if you tend to be more introverted and just want to eat, listen to a podcast, and be in your own thoughts.

Whenever he'd leave his room, Brian would feel a strong pressure to engage with others and entertain them. He imagined if he didn't do this, he simply made his food and ate in silence, enjoying his own company that other housemates would think he was awkward, anti-social, and generally unlikeable.

To help Brian overcome this fear, we practiced a powerful technique I learned in my clinical training from one of the top cognitive therapists in the world, Dr. David Burns. In this technique, called the Feared Fantasy, you imagine that instead of your housemates (or whoever you are worried will judge you) are just thinking negative things, you actually imagine that they walk up to you and say those judgments. Then you practice responding to them.

The purpose of this exercise is to provide exposure to these fears, learn to deal with them, and ultimately to strengthen your sense of your rules, how you want to live, and self-acceptance. For short, I call this "owning your reality."

So here's how the role play went:

HOUSEMATE: Hey Brian

BRIAN: Hey Leon

HOUSEMATE: What are you doing over here all by yourself?

BRIAN: Just eating some dinner and listening to a podcast.

HOUSEMATE: Oh… that's kinda weird isn't it?

BRIAN: I don't know…

HOUSEMATE: Why are you being all antisocial? You should come out with us and drink on the patio.

BRIAN: Nah, I'm good, man.

HOUSEMATE: Who listens to podcasts anyway?

At this point, Brian broke from the role play and said he was getting angry and would most likely fire back with a sharp or cutting comment. I highlighted that this is not surprising as this imaginary housemate is indeed being a jerk. Anger might be an appropriate response!

And, the truth is we're not dealing with a housemate. We're dealing with the internal criticisms that Brian launches against himself. That's so important; it's worth highlighting again, but making it clearly about you instead of Brian. **The criticisms you imagine others have of you are actually your own judgments of yourself.** It's your own self-dislike projected out onto the minds of others, also known as "projected dislike."

You have some pressure of how you're supposed to be that came from the programming in your upbringing and in the cultural field in which you grew up and live now. Brian is supposed to be outgoing, loud, funny, engaging, and entertaining. Always.

Maybe his mom expected that of him when he was young. Heck, she may have even said, you need to be this way, and if you're not, I think you're bad, and I don't love you. Which, obviously, would be extremely painful for a young child.

I've had clients tell me their parents or aunts or grandparents have told them as much, in no uncertain terms. Top-notch parenting and child-raising there, eh? But that's just that one person expressing their view of the reality of how their kid, or people in general, "should" be.

Now, in this present moment, the only one putting this pressure on Brian is, well, Brian. It's that internalized voice in his head that is constantly leaning on him to be this certain way that he learned a long, long time ago is the "right" way to be.

To put it another way, Brian is still predominantly living in his mom's reality. And it's time to break free. So we did the role play again, but this time, Brian played his housemate and I played Brian so I could model how to create space between you and these critical voices. The key is to be curious about their perception of reality, allowing yourself to differentiate and share where you agree or disagree with it. In this way, you get to claim your own reality, which might be different than your inner critics.

BRIAN (as housemate): Hey Brian

AZIZ (as Brian): Hey Leon, how's it going man?

BRIAN: Just chillin'. Hey, what are you doing over here all by yourself?

AZIZ: I'm eating some delicious food I just cooked up and listening to a great podcast.

BRIAN: All by yourself? Isn't that a little weird?

AZIZ: Oh…maybe. I actually really love some down time and space. I spend a lot of my day working with people and it feels really good to just be in my own space and thoughts for a while.

BRIAN: Huh. That seems kind of awkward to me.

AZIZ: Really? That's fascinating? Do you never have solo time?

BRIAN: Nah, not really man. Why be all awkward by yourself listening to a podcast? Besides, who listens to podcasts man?

AZIZ: Haha, I thought everyone! Seriously you never listen to a book or podcast or anything? I love that stuff! I listen to something interesting or educational at least once a day. I love learning and growing. What do you listen to?

BRIAN: Music man. Cool music. Like trap and hip-hop.

AZIZ: Well touché, that does seem cooler. *(laughs)*

After we paused this role-play, I asked Brian and the other group members what they noticed. I'll ask you the same. What do you notice about how I am with this imaginary critic? What stands out to you about how I am being and responding?

Notice how I am able to own my own preferences, interests, and likes. I am able to own that I enjoy the podcast I'm listening to and that I love learning in general. If someone criticizes that and says that's nerdy or stupid or wrong or bad or... I can simply get curious. I mean, I truly would be curious! *Really? Learning is stupid? Huh, I never thought of that perspective. Tell me more, what's stupid about it?*

There's also the ability to accept the truth in certain statements without needing to take on the judgemental charge. If the housemate accuses me of sitting there all by myself, I can simply agree that I'm there by myself. He may load that with judgment, but I don't have to. I simply acknowledge what is so.

This is where we get into the strengthening of your reality. In my reality it's okay to eat alone. It's okay to listen to podcasts, in fact I enjoy them! It's okay to eat whatever I'm eating. It's okay to not want to be outside drinking on the patio.

This would be a great time for you to do a quick strengthening exercise for your reality. Simply write out some of the things that you believe, enjoy, and want to do in your life. And write each one out starting with the phrase, "in my reality…"

Be sure to include things that you perhaps learned in the past were embarrassing, uncool, or somehow not what others would have liked or wanted in the past. So if your family thought that emotions were weak, then in your reality, claim something about how it's okay to feel.

Here's a quick example list:

In my reality it's okay to say no to someone's request (even if they have feelings about it!)

In my reality it's okay to disagree.

In my reality it's okay to feel scared, anxious, or upset.

In my reality it's okay to take time off (or time purely for myself).

In my reality it's okay to try new things, take risks, make mistakes, and fail.

In my reality it's okay to enjoy fantasy, sci-fi, and Magic: The Gathering.

I could go on and on, and perhaps you will! Once you get writing, it might feel good, and the permission will just start pouring out. Breathe in and out fully as you write, expanding your chest and body, claiming this new reality. Better yet, once you've written it all down on paper or digitally, stand up in your room and read it out loud. Proclaim it!

It can also be extremely beneficial to practice the kind of role-play I did with Brian in the group. You can enlist the help of a friend or family member and let them know you'd like to overcome a fear of someone judging you. Then coach them on how you imagine someone would think negatively about you in a certain situation and practice with them.

If you don't have anyone you'd want to do this with, you can do it on paper, where you simply write both sides of the interaction, like a play or movie script. In-person with another human is often more powerful, so do that if you can; otherwise, the paper version can work as well.

If you're interested in participating in coaching with me and the mastermind group, you can visit draziz.com to learn more and watch countless videos of clients just like you sharing their breakthroughs and success stories.

To conclude this chapter, I'd like to share one humorous story of some hefty disapproval coming my way in which the feared fantasy wasn't just in my head but someone actually said these things out loud to me.

Having practiced the technique hundreds of times myself and with clients, I was amazed when I simply engaged in the conversation out loud, using the exact same approach.

I was at a house poker game organized by one of my friends. It was a way to connect, meet new people, and of course, win some caassh. As we were playing, my friend spontaneously mentioned to me, "By the way, I started listening to some Tony Robbins interviews and materials online. I'd never listened to him before. It was surprisingly useful."

My friend knew that I was an author and a coach and had heard about some of my experiences at Tony's live events, which were very positive and beneficial for me.

Another man at the table, who I had only met an hour earlier when I arrived, spoke up immediately.

"Pssh, Tony Robbins," he said with clear disdain. "That guy just takes money from gullible people who are desperate."

This man didn't know what I did for a living, or that I had attended some of Tony's events. At that moment, I could have been defensive, or felt the need to protect something. But I was rooted in my reality. I know that those events were beneficial for me, and I'd seen the teaching and coaching I'd provided over the years powerfully change so many lives. So instead of defending myself, I simply asked him some questions.

"What of Tony's materials have you read or watched?" I asked.

"None," he scoffed.

"Oh." I replied. I let this sit for a moment because I was surprised. I imagined he would've had some contact to have that strong of an opinion.

"I'm curious," I said. "If someone had a challenge that they were struggling to overcome, and they tried everything they could think of to beat it, but weren't able to, what do you think they should do?"

"Nothing a six pack of beer in the back yard wouldn't handle," he said with a wry grin on his face.

"Fair enough," I replied, letting the conversation drop.

I don't know all the details of this guy's reality, but it sure is not the one that I would want to inhabit.

So let me ask you — whose reality have you been inhabiting, and do you like it there? How long have you been letting that dominate your perspective and make you feel scared or inadequate? When are you going to claim something new? A reality that actually fits you, that honors your gifts and your natural passion, essence, and desires in this life? When are you going to give yourself complete permission to be who you really are, and then celebrate that?

When you do this, you'll be drinking a big swig off that liberation tonic. Drink regularly throughout the day for an optimal feeling of vigor and well-being.

CHAPTER 42

I AM NOT YOUR FRIEND

As you release the pressure to have everyone like you, you also release the pressure for you to like everyone else, and the pressure to pretend to like everyone else (which is even worse).

One simple line I remind myself with prior to dealings in which I will need to be more assertive — in business, with contractors, home matters, etc. — I remind myself of this simple line: "I am not your friend."

Now, I don't come out and start the conversation that way, that would be way too awkward. "Listen pal, I don't like you and you don't like me…"

Instead, this is a simple mantra to use internally before and during an interaction in which you are prone to fall into nice-mode. In the last year, we moved into our dream home in the woods, which involved dealing with a lot of other people, from real estate agents and brokers, to contractors, builders, and inspectors, to neighbors, and community members.

I tend to have a warm, friendly disposition and enjoy connecting with others. This is partly my natural personality, and also partly a muscle that I keep toned through practice. I know that my history of social anxiety and niceness can easily lead me to be withdrawn and avoidant of people, which doesn't actually make me feel good in the long run or live out a meaningful life. So, when I'm in the mood, I'll ask people questions, genuinely listen to them, and deeply connect with them.

But, I also can run a nice guy pattern in which I'm doing these things but don't actually want to, which is bad. I can also do this with someone who I'm paying or otherwise dealing with for other purposes, such as moving, which is superbad. For example, if I'm hiring a handyman to help me install some light fixtures in a property I'm selling, I'm not there to hang out or connect with them. That might happen, but ultimately, I'm there to get light fixtures installed.

But what if the guy shows up late? What if he's unreliable? What if he's all talky-pants and takes a long time to do the job because he's talking to me so much, but he's getting paid by the hour? What do you do in this situation? Listen and nod and smile? Keep the conversation going? Avoiding calling him out on being late?

I sure did… Until I didn't.

And this magic mantra is the key: I am not your friend.

I started saying this to myself before dealing with anyone related to this house. I might be friendly or warm, but ultimately I'm not their friend, and I don't need to be. That's not my role in their life. This reminds me what I really am interacting with them for — to get a job done. This is a transaction.

Now, you can find all kinds of personal development, spiritual, and new age teachings that say transactional interactions are bad, that we need to open our hearts and connect with others, soul to soul, or that the world is so bad because we don't look the cashier in the eye and ask them with earnest sincerity, "How are you today?"

I don't know about all that. All I know is that when a nice person interacts with someone and doesn't keep it transactional, they get screwed. At least, I sure did. So I began using this mantra to prep myself before the interaction. This primed me to remove many of the social graces and empathic interaction that I would have with a friend or client, in which my outcome is to create a deep connection.

So when my contractor starts telling me about his daughter or his sick mother in law, I had to learn how to respond without much empathy. It felt so strange and bad at first. *What kind of monster am I?? The man's mother-in-law is dying for God's sake!*

But if I responded with empathy, warmth, and curiosity, like I would with a friend, he'd just keep talking. I mean, he could go on about it for an hour. During the entire time we were supposed to be talking about fixing the leak issues in the new roof. And then nothing progresses and water is leaking into our kids bedroom ceiling. But at least I was a good, nice person when I talked with him.

Barf to being a good person, and double barf to pretending to be friends with everyone. It might feel bad to override those friendly, warm ways of interacting, but it feels way worse to be walked all over, pay more, and be a doormat sponge in this life.

So now, when he tells me about his dying mother in law, I subdue any warmth in my voice and make a single statement about the topic and immediately switch subjects.

"That sounds rough, I'm sorry to hear that. I have a question about the trim around this door I'd like to ask you about…"

Yep, just like that. I know it sounds bad, but to me, it sounds like freedom.

When I remember I'm not someone's friend, my entire tone, demeanor and attitude changes. My options of what to say and how to say it expand radically. I can call things out quickly and directly and ask them why something wasn't completed.

Here's a fresh example just from this week:

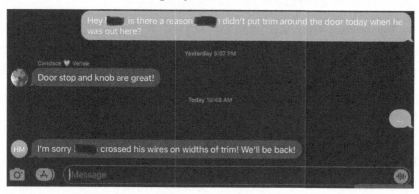

Our contractor was going to have one of his guys come and complete an outside door that had been unaddressed for more than a month, creating what my wife referred to as a "rodent superhighway" into our house. Why so long? Well, it turns out if you're pretending to be friends with people, things don't get done.

Within the last few weeks I've completely changed my tone and interaction style, removing all friend role energy. Our contractor told us a date his guy would come out, but he didn't. I immediately emailed saying "When you tell us someone will be there and they aren't, and you don't alert me as to why or when it will be rescheduled, it erodes my trust. When will he actually come out here?"

Now, the guy did finally come out here and put the door knob on, but didn't do the trim, which would stop the rodent highway. When I found out, I immediately texted that message in the light gray at the top. My wife added the second message most likely because she was uncomfortable with my "zero-friend vibes" approach. At first I didn't want to make her uncomfortable either so I'd soften my statements and still be friendly. But no more.

After no response for a day and a half, my follow up was that fine specimen you see above... the triple dots. Which in my mind means *I'm waiting for a response you owe me from my last message*.

Notice how he ignored the first message, including the friendly tone from Candace. He responded to the triple dot message within 20 minutes.

So what's the lesson here? Be a jerk to those you hire? No, certainly not. My messages are all direct, but still respectful. I don't call him names, disparage him, or otherwise insult him. I just say what needs to be said, and remove the false tone of artificial warmth and friendship.

Not only does that feel terrible to you inside afterward, it is also radically less effective.

So the next time you're dealing with the airline attendant, or your dentist, or a dude coming to fix a broken pipe in your house, take a moment to remind yourself, *I am not your friend*, and then watch in delight at the powerful, assertive version of you that emerges.

CHAPTER 43

FROZEN IN TIME

Not too long ago, miners digging for gold in the Yukon permafrost of Canada came across a strange object. After removing a huge chunk of ice and inspecting what was within, they discovered the most well-preserved, complete baby mammoth in North America. The little creature was dubbed Nun Cho Ga, which means "big baby animal" in the Han language and was rushed off by paleontologists for further study.

Despite being an interesting factoid to share at the next party you go to, this little story has specific relevance to you. Because every nice person I know is attempting to minimize conflict in their life because it feels painful and counterproductive. They perceive conflict as being something bad that should be avoided, and if you're doing your relationships and your life "right," then it won't happen.

But this way of seeing conflict, also known as direct contact, is severely limiting — not just for your relationships but actually for your own growth, authenticity, personal development, and even spiritual evolution.

This hindrance is due to the way avoiding conflict tends to freeze us in time. If you are upset with a spouse, parent, colleague, or friend and you avoid the conversation that needs to be had, choosing instead to stew in silence, the freezing process begins. All that hurt, upset, or anger gets buried underground, where it gets stuck. In the words of a book with a great title: feelings buried alive never die.

So now the way you feel and all the perspectives you have about the situation get crusty and frozen, becoming hard to change and update. You thought your ex-husband was a jerk ten years ago, and now, ten years later, you think your ex-husband is a jerk. All that hurt and upset is still there, just frozen in time. Your mom is still mean, your dad is still uncaring, your colleague is still an achievement-seeking self-centered piece of... well, you get my point.

Like that frozen little mammoth, Nun Cho Ga, all your feelings and perspectives get stuck and just stay there. (Hopefully, not as long as he was frozen in that ice, which was around 30,000 years).

But I'm afraid it will get worse. Because without conflict, you will also greatly hinder your own growth. This limits your ability to reach your potential, feel happy, give and receive more love, and achieve all that you want to achieve in this life. It turns out that conflict is often the catalyst that's needed to spur you forward in life.

By going into the upset and expressing it out loud, you radically increase the flow of new information and perspectives. Perhaps when you challenge your colleague or speak up with your mom, they say something back. Maybe, God forbid, you have a fight! How awful!

Or is it?

Does the fight break up frozen ice? Does the heat of the expressed anger allow energy to start flowing again so that you can update your perspectives and experience new feelings?

You might think that all fights are inherently unproductive and bad. And sure, there is a way in which two people hurling character attacks at each other with absolutely no real communication can be unhelpful. But that is just one far end of the extreme. There are many shades of gray here in which you can speak up, have direct conflict, passionately express differing views, get upset with each other, and then leave the situation so much better for it.

Perhaps it's very uncomfortable for a day, or even a week or two. It can be painful or scary to swim out in the uncertain waters of the edge of the unknown. Not sure what you or the other person wants, not sure how it will all resolve. But if you keep with it, keep discovering, sharing what you see, and saying the next thing that seems true at that moment, the storm passes, and you find something extraordinary beyond.

What if your next breakthrough to a new level of confidence, power, authenticity, and freedom didn't lie in a book, a podcast, or a spiritual teaching? What if it emerged from your next fight?

CHAPTER 44

A Fight In The Kitchen

I had a hard time making eye contact with Candace. I glanced at her, seeing the tears in her eyes, then looked down at the deep green stone tiles of our kitchen. I felt an invisible force field that compelled me to move away, create distance, and find safety in solitude. I didn't want her this close.

To make matters worse, she had just shared vulnerably about how painful it was for her when I got upset and withdrew, as I was doing at that very moment. And to make matters double worse, everything she was pointing out about my blocks to intimacy and my immaturity was true.

I couldn't even get on the moral high ground of "I'm right and you're wrong," which is a highly sought-after and oh-so-common maneuver in fights between couples.

While I had radically grown in my capacity for deep intimacy over the last twelve years that we'd been together, we had just entered a new level, and I was thrashing against it. Not the sexy level of new lovers or the sweet level of new parents raising a newborn. No, this was a new level of intimacy brought on by a medical problem (yuck)...in my penis (double yuck).

A number of months before this fight in the kitchen, my eight-year-old son and I had been playing with foam bats that are meant for swordplay. Being the master swashbuckler that I am, I dodged one of his sideswipes by jumping backward. However, at that exact moment, the stars were aligned in such a way that the tip of his foam bat swiped the tip of my penis with extreme force. Thereby, well, breaking it. No, not the foam bat, I'm afraid.

What followed was many visits to many urologists, most of whom said there were no options other than to wait for the scar tissue to form, the "penile deformities" to complete, and then to do surgery. Side note, if breaking your penis is not hard enough on the ego, waiting for "penile deformities to complete" will do wonders for your confidence.

I'll spare you from my tales of medical woe, but the short version is that there are interventions that can be done to repair and potentially reverse the damage without surgery; you just have to find the right doctors. And guess who found that? That's right, Candace.

Because up until that point, I had dealt with the situation by generally avoiding it and hoping it would all work out for the best. Solid plan.

Flash forward to now, and I was about to fly to Chicago to see a specialist who was going to inject my penis with magical drugs to help prevent further scar tissue and deformities from forming. It was my first trip of at least six in which I'd have to fly out there from my home in Oregon... once every two weeks for six months.

Two days before the trip, I was a mess. I didn't want to go, but I didn't want to not pursue treatment either. I was angry and resistant to having to deal with it. My sense of masculine pride was shattered, and I felt like an infirmed old man whose wife had to help him go to the bathroom. Of course, this wasn't the exact scenario, but there was an element of intimacy and vulnerability that was beyond what I've experienced. And beyond what I wanted.

When I was deep in the cage of niceness, I believed anger, conflict, and any sort of fighting were bad. I imagined I was a spiritually evolved guy who was able to quickly dispel my anger on my own and live in peace and love with others. Never mind that I didn't have any deep relationships, and I couldn't date a woman longer than three months. Those have nothing to do with each other!

As I discovered what you are learning in this book, I began to realize that conflict — although generally unpleasant — is an essential ingredient to a thriving relationship. In fact, in order to experience deep intimacy, trust, passion, and lasting love, we must have conflict now and then to clear the air and break through to the next level of connection.

You see, all of us have layers of armor around our hearts. Even people who consider themselves "an open book" often have places they don't want to go and don't want others to go. Part of deepening our relationships and living a life of authenticity involves softening and taking our defenses down with those closest to us.

While you might want this to occur peacefully over a candle-lit dinner in which you both vulnerably share while holding each other in total love and compassion... it might not always go this way. Sometimes it's a fight in the kitchen where you're both standing on opposite sides of the island countertop, feeling heat inside, hurting, thrashing against the very person closest to you. Because true authenticity and deep relationships are messy, raw, and real.

This kind of conflict isn't bad. It's growth.

I saw Candace crying. I'd been irritable and pushed her away every time this topic had come up for weeks. I knew I should go to her and reassure her. But I couldn't do it. I didn't want to override that feeling and go act like the good husband. More truth was needed instead of pretending or playing the role.

So I shared about how challenging it was for me to lose that masculine independence, to have my penis poked and prodded and discussed by her and doctors and receptionists and pharmacists. I know it's a level of intimacy that is part of a life-long relationship. I know that we're both going to get old and sick and that we're deeply committed to being with each other through all the seasons of life.

"But," I said, now able to look at her directly as I said what needed to be said, "my initial response to this is not to soften and open, it's to harden and withdraw. I'm not saying I stand by it or I'm going to stay here. I do ultimately want this level of intimacy and a life together at the deepest levels… It's just going to take a bit for me to get there. I have more to discover, more to heal, more to let go."

Over the next few days after this heated exchange, something softened in me. I saw how my pride that wanted to push Candace away was born out of a fear of letting her get in so close. Beneath the persona of Aziz, who is warm and upbeat and funny and charming, a capable, healthy man, is the Aziz, who is sometimes sick, weak, or running from facing his challenges, who is irrational, scared, and upset — the Aziz who has penile deformities that will (hopefully) heal.

I can see why I didn't want Candace to get to know that version of me. Heck, I don't even like hanging out with him. He's so… weak and gross. I feel waves of aversion just being aware of him myself, let alone letting Candace or you see him.

But I'm not here to be comfortable or preserve some image of myself. I'm here to be real. I'm here to be seen and known and offer everything I have to serve at the most powerful level while I'm still on this planet.

Over the next few days I had insight after insight about the ways I defended myself from Candace, from those close to me, and from life. Layers of armor melted away, and I became more able to talk vulnerably and openly about my challenging feelings during the medical process. Not only was this significant for my own growth and my relationship, it was also great preparation for a future in which we will all get old, experience sickness, and eventually die. Good preparation to start softening and expanding our capacities now, right?

So, my friend, the next time you are about to have a fight in the kitchen, instead of staying silent and withdrawing to stew in your own anger for weeks, instead of adding another layer of ice to that two-mile-deep permafrost… maybe you need to have the conversation you don't want to have. It might just be the magic ingredient to bring you to an entirely new level of confidence, self-acceptance, and freedom.

CHAPTER 45

IF I WASN'T HOLDING BACK

What would you say if you weren't holding anything back? That is a powerful question to ponder. What would you say in your romantic relationship? With family? At work? With clients or colleagues or your boss?

At first you might scoff at this question, writing it off as unrealistic. *It doesn't really even matter what I'd say because there's no way I could say it anyway. It's unacceptable, risky, and just something you don't do...*

Really? How do you know? Besides, even if you choose not to say it exactly as it comes to you at this moment, is there still a key essence you'd like to communicate, perhaps with more tact?

I find most people are scared to even ask themselves this question for fear of what it might bring up. *Maybe I'd feel anger with someone close to me, or see the places I'm dissatisfied with my career.* This question cuts through denial and avoidance and helps you see what you really want to say, and ultimately who you really want to be and what you want to do with this one wild, crazy life.

You can ask yourself this question when you notice you're feeling agitated, anxious, or irritated after leaving a meeting, a date, or time with a family member. If you weren't holding back at all, and you didn't need to say it right, preserve their feelings or follow the culture of avoidance and walking on eggshells that may have developed, what would you say?

At first, it might come out as highly judgmental, blaming, or even attacking. That's ok. You don't need to be afraid of these feelings. They're just feelings, and they won't destroy you or others.

In fact, I often recommend clients give themselves space and time to really go with these feelings. For this, I utilize a simple yet very powerful technique from Gestalt therapy called "the Open Chair." To practice this, sit opposite an empty chair and imagine the person that you have unfinished business with sitting across from you. Then start talking to them. You say all that you've never said, all that you want to say, all that you need to say for your sense of sanity and the freedom of your soul.

Tell them what you disagree with, what you're angry and hurting about. Tell them what you want, your frustrations, your worries and your concerns. Tell them everything you need to tell them. Hold nothing back.

This exercise begins the thawing out process of all those buried, frozen feelings and stuck perspectives. If there are a lot of emotional charges there, I will suggest clients practice this multiple times per week, often with the same imagined person. You don't always have to literally be sitting across from an empty chair. Once you get the hang of it, you can practice this anywhere. I will often have these "conversations" while out for a long run in the woods. One of my clients told me the empty chair was in the passenger seat next to her during her long morning commute.

Once you've begun to clear the festering and frozen feelings, rage, and sludge, you can explore what you might actually want to say to certain people in your life. You can determine how polished you make the actual conversation, but let me give you a few pointers from having done this process myself and with hundreds of clients.

First, no matter how polished you try to be by planning it all out ahead of time, the only thing you really can plan is your opening lines. Once the conversation is underway, it has a life of its own, and it's best to not try and stick to a predetermined script. Instead, actually, be with the other person or people on the razor's edge of the present moment.

This makes the exchange a dialogue in which you're actually seeing and hearing the person in front of you. You can let new information in, update your perspectives, and truly connect instead of simply reinforcing an old story you have about you, them, and "how it is."

Secondly, you don't really need to polish things up that much. Often when I ask clients what they'd say if they weren't holding back, they take a big breath, let out a heavy sigh and then unburden themselves of their buried truths. Afterward, they'll cringe at imagining how bad that sounds and how awful it would be to say it to their friend, mom, boss, or partner.

In the vast majority of cases, what they say is direct, real, and honest. It's blunt, for sure, but it is in no way disrespectful or unacceptable to say. Here are a few examples of things that clients have shared that they imagine would be too harsh to say and would instead need to be watered down or sugar-coated:

"I expect you to be on time for every shift and if you're not I'm going to give you a warning. After three warnings, I'll need to let you go."

"You always say how much you love me, but when I share about myself and my life you don't seem very interested."

"I want something different in our sex life. It's not bad… it's just not great. I want so much more."

How would you feel saying these kinds of statements? Would it be easy? Edgy? You might be thinking: *Aziz, these kinds of statements are pussy cats… if I were to speak up and say what I really think, it would be so much worse!*

Perhaps. Remember, it might start with you ranting and raving at an empty chair. But when you sit down to think about what you might actually want to say without holding back after you've cleared some of the initial sludge and resentment, what would you want to say?

I've also helped many clients enhance what they'd say to make it much more effective at getting their point across and forging new connections. For example, if someone's initial desire would be to say:

"I'm sick of hearing about all the details of your work. It's absolutely boring and a waste of time."

Then I'd start by asking what is the purpose of this communication? Do you want to be closer to this person? Do you want them to talk about something else? Do you want them to share more depth in their experience rather than just the superficial details? Do you want them to be more interested in you and your life? What do you really want here?

If you are hurting and angry and you want to express that, you can do so in a way that is taking more ownership and fewer blamey-pants statements. This will not only feel better for you, but it will also increase your assertiveness skills and self-esteem. In that case, you could upgrade this statement to:

"I notice that when you talk about the details of your work, I have a hard time staying engaged. I've been forcing myself to pay attention and have found that to be effortful and agitating."

Notice the frequent use of "I" language. What you have been doing and what you need to be different.

Just remember that you don't need to do any of this perfectly. Assertiveness is never completely polished and perfect. It's messy and real. And that's what makes it so meaningful and alive.

The final pointer is to remember that we are all affected by each other and our conversations. The more direct, deep, and real the conversation, the more it impacts us.

I'll never forget a conversation I had with Candace on the couch at our old house right after our second son was born. At the time, we were two months away from moving into another house, which was being remodeled and needed constant management to deal with issues, including large amounts of toxic lead dust. I was running a business and taking on the responsibilities that come with a new baby entering the home.

And I was being a bit pouty about it all, I must admit. I'd often have an attitude of exasperation with the demands on me, huffing and puffing around the house.

One night after the kids were asleep, Candace sat me down on the couch and, in direct terms, told me she needed more from me right now. Not just me doing more actions… I was doing quite a lot already and handling all that needed to be handled. What she needed was for me to fully show up to the demands of this season of life with more ownership and more maturity. Here's the line I'll never forget:

"Instead of being the dad, it's like you're being older brother Aziz. Like a teenager who has to take care of his younger siblings and hates doing it."

As soon as she said this, I laughed. It was so accurate. We even started joking about a teenager and all the things he'd say and do in exasperation when his parents asked him to take care of his baby brother.

And so I grew. No, it didn't happen instantly, but the seed was planted. I examined where I was making myself the victim of the circumstances and therefore resenting responsibilities in my life. I reminded myself daily that I chose this, and I continue to choose it.

We deeply desired to have a second child. In fact, his name Arman means "the heart's deepest desire." Within a short period, I'd stepped up to the challenge and resumed my place as the dad, only going to teenage Aziz for brief moments here and there.

I wonder what might change in your life and in your relationships when you start saying what needs to be said. Whose life besides your own will be profoundly impacted by you not holding back?

CHAPTER 46

DYING OF REGRET

Remember way back at the start of this book when you discovered the number one regret of the dying? It turns out that there's more than just one, you know. People often die with all kinds of regrets, wishing they'd done different things with their time, made different decisions, or even been a different person.

While this might sound sad, the problem is it can still seem so distant, so far off. Most likely, you're not dying as you read this. I mean, there's plenty of time. Certainly, you won't be one of those people, who's riddled with regret as they die, right?

But the truth is, the regrets aren't just hovering around the deathbed. The regrets are right here and right now. Most clients I talk with are experiencing a significant amount of pain about the life they're currently not living, what they've missed out on so far, and what they will miss out on next.

When I was living in the cage of niceness and social anxiety, it felt like I was on the sidelines of my own life. A second-string player on the bench, or maybe even simply a fan in the distant bleachers. Other people were the ones who could be out on the field, under the spotlights, living fully. Dating, exciting adventures, and a confident life were all for other people.

I remember one evening, somewhere in my decades in the cage, when I went to see a movie with a friend. It was a fast-paced, action comedy about beautiful people in their twenties and thirties having wild adventures, road trips to Vegas, drug deals, all-night raves, and a car chase or two.

It was awesome... until the movie ended. As the theater lights slowly turned back on, the energizing euphoria of watching the movie passed, and I was left with a depressing sadness. I didn't need my life to be an over-the-top, unrealistic drama. But I wasn't sad about that. I was sad because so many of the things those characters were doing seemed out of reach to me:meeting new people, dating, parties, adventures... all of it seemed off limits. It was out on the field, and there I was, stuck in the bleachers behind the fence.

Years later, as I began working with clients, I discovered these feelings weren't unique to me. Many people at this very moment are living on the sidelines of their own lives, living in a fantasy of "someday maybe" doing those things that would make them feel more alive, or sadly resigning themselves to a life that is not fully their own, and certainly not what they would enthusiastically call extraordinary.

One day I was speaking with a client who was way up in the bleachers of their own life — struggling with old friendships that no longer served her, afraid to make new friends because of stories of her own inadequacy, working a job she didn't love but feeling too afraid to make a change, struggling to create real intimacy with a partner she wasn't sure was right for her — and it hit me... She's not going to experience some regret later on her deathbed; she's living a life of regret right now. Or perhaps not really even living. Sort of living, sort of dying. Dying of regret.

This kind of dying might not stop you from breathing or shut down your body. But it will stop you from dreaming and shut down your heart. It will turn the world from the bright, fresh, expansive field of possibility that you may have felt as a young child and turn it into a long slog, a death march of sorts, depressing, draining, and seemingly endless.

Dying of regret doesn't kill your body, it kills your soul — it's death by a thousand paper cuts. A little avoidance here, a little holding back there. Smiling when you want to cry, or scream. The conversation you didn't have. The real feelings you held back. The missed opportunity, missed conversation, missed date. Letting your potential mate and life partner walk passed because you're too scared to strike up a conversation.

Heart disease, cancer, and strokes got nothing on death by regret. Those diseases and ailments take millions of lives every year, but a life not fully lived and the regret that ensues takes its toll in the billions.

As you've been reading this book you hopefully have felt both challenged and inspired, agitated and energized. But it's all too easy to go on the adventure ride that is this book, and then return to the parking lot, back to "normal life."

And if you do that, then I've failed. I've failed in my goal to agitate you into action. To spark the fire in your soul that has you fiercely claim something more, pushing off the familiar shores of safety into the wild, unpredictable, glorious unknown.

The choice is yours my friend, what are you going to do when you put this book down?

> *I'm tired of sailing my little boat*
> *Far inside of the harbor bar;*
> *I want to be out where the big ships float —*
> *Out on the deep where the Great Ones are!...*
> *And should my frail craft prove too slight*
> *For storms that sweep those wide seas o'er,*
> *Better go down in the stirring fight*
> *Than drowse to death by the sheltered shore!*
> — Daisy Rinehart

CHAPTER 47

6,497

That's how many experiences you'll have. Exactly six thousand, four hundred and ninety seven.

Okay, that number might vary depending on how old you are and what you deem a "life-experience." But for most of us, there are sections of our day that are not that memorable where everything just blurs together. And then there's a day where you have "an experience." You know what I'm talking about?

Just this last weekend my older son had his first sleepover with a friend. It was epic. They played outside, stayed up late watching a movie, ate pizza and slept on sleeping bags in the family room. The next morning they woke up early, played more, ate pancakes, and made "God weapons" (that yours truly spray painted with metallic gold and silver spray paints because I'm an awesome dad).

After his friend left my son moped around the rest of the day, saying how fun it had been. That was no ordinary Friday night… that was an experience!

However you slice it, you, me, and all of us have a finite number of these experiences. Some are going to be epic, fun, and memorable, like your first sleepover, falling in love, a great trip to a new city, or achieving a major goal in your life. Others are going to be memorable for an entirely different reason; they'll bring loss, pain, or disturbance to your life.

We all like the first kind and attempt to avoid the latter. Or, in the words of a little song my wife came up with one day when we were talking on our patio, and I was lamenting some ill fortune: "Give me the good, don't give me any bad... I want the good, take away the bad."

And yet we're all going to get a mixture, aren't we?

This is a fixed and unavoidable part of existence, it would seem. Despite your best attempts to say things in just the right way, take all the right actions, and optimize everything... you still can't get away from some of that bad.

Furthermore, the more authentic and bold you become, the more risks you'll take. Some of those will lead to amazing outcomes such as love, success, wealth, and increased opportunity. And others will lead to pain, loss, and undesirable consequences.

So what are you going to do in this predicament?

After spending years grasping for "good" and being chronically stressed about the "bad" looming around the corner, I decided to surrender in a more complete way. This took the form of The Ultimate Checklist. Let me explain.

This checklist has a good column and a bad column. Obviously, life has a lot more nuance and gradation than this, but I like it simple.

When I have an amazing experience, I attempt to really savor it, taking in the positivity, joy, and aliveness it brings. I savor the preciousness, and even some of the tender sadness that is mixed with the joy, knowing this experience is temporary and the moment will pass.

First dates with the love of my life where the whole world stopped, and electrical currents of energy zinged through my nervous system and scrambled my brain. Moments of passion and deep meaning beyond words. Check.

Holding my son's little hand when he was a toddler as he walked down the road, pointing out flowers and kittens. So sweet it makes me smile, laugh, and cry at the same time. Check.

Spending a day running around a mountain by myself from dawn to darkness, seeing no one. Crossing streams, crunching across the desolate pumice fields of The Plains of Abraham, and hearing volcanic boulders tumble and move in a deep valley below like the spine of an ancient stone dragon slowly awakening from its slumber. As the sun sets, I'm running through the forest crying with joy, the experience being that much more majestic for all the years I spent in chronic pain, thinking I would never run again. Check.

Pretty sweet, huh? Well it turns out I have a bunch of experiences in the bad column as well:

Embarrassed myself horribly while attempting to start a conversation with a stranger. Check. Let's give that one a lot of checks actually.

Fallen in love so hard I didn't know which way was up and then had my heart broken into a million pieces. Check.

Lost a bunch of money to a super crafty, super convincing con man. Check.

Hated myself for many years, then dealt with that self-loathing by being harsh, critical, and kind of a terrible person in many ways. Check.

Suffered from chronic pain and hopelessness about my physical abilities for twenty years. Check.

Well, now, we can stop there. That list is probably a bit less inspiring. But guess what? I wouldn't change a thing.

This is it. This is what we get. This is our only certain experience of life on this planet. Perhaps you come back again and again in the great wheel of reincarnation, or go to some super awesome pleasure-filled heaven realm, or who knows what after this.

But in the meantime, we have today. Right now. How many experiences will you have today? One? Three? What check boxes will you mark?

Instead of dreading something that might go wrong, expect that things will go wrong. Bad things will happen. And boy, won't that be another experience to add to your list. And then, in between those bad ones, there sure is so much to add to your good column, isn't there?

Because instead of having to wait for an epic once-in-a-lifetime kind of event to check a box in your good column, what if you could slow down to see the beauty in five moments from just today?

What if the twinkle in your partner's eye, or the soft fur of your cat in your lap, or the sound of the rain on the roof was an extraordinary experience?

Because whether you call them good or bad, embrace them or resist them, increase or decrease the number based on how you count them, one fact remains my friend.

You only have so many left.

I wanna taste love and pain
Wanna feel pride and shame
I don't wanna take my time
Don't wanna waste one line
I wanna live better days
Never look back and say
Could have been me
It could have been me

— Could Have Been Me by The Struts

CHAPTER 48

NOW

Wearing my swimming trunks, I walked in my sandals alongside my two boys, dogs in tow, towards the lake. The late winter rain was no longer the icy droplets it once was, and spring was coming but hadn't quite arrived. Regardless, we were dressed like it was a hot July day at the beach. Why?

Wim Hoff!

He's an international sensation, so you probably have heard of him by now. If not, take a moment to Youtube that crazy Dutchman, and you'll see why he's so popular. A humble, quirky, and deeply inspiring man with a passion for encouraging people to be and do more than they thought they could... specifically, using deliberate cold exposure.

Hence the walk to the lake in the cold rain. But that was just the beginning. The lake itself was about 45 degrees, which might not sound that cold, but if you've ever submerged in water at that temperature... it's something else.

As we approached the oversized pond at the bottom of our forest (calling it a lake is somewhat ambitious), my younger son started to moan. He had said he wanted to go into the water back at the house, which is why we began walking down in the first place. I told him if he wanted to do it, I'd do it with him.

But now, as the lake came into view, the dread began in force.

"I don't really want to do it," he said, matter-of-factly.

"Yeah, me too," I laughed. "But I know that dread pretty much always comes before doing anything meaningful or extraordinary."

He didn't say anything more until we got down to the water.

I'd learned from my two decades of boldness practice what to do in this situation: throw the towel over a tree branch, kick off the sandals, and get in the water as quickly as possible. Hesitating by the side of the lake was a breeding ground for dread and doubt to massively delay, or possibly completely halt the endeavor. I'd done enough of that dance in my years in the cage and since made a habit of constantly practicing immediate bold action, especially when I don't want to do something that's beneficial or meaningful.

The edge of the water was covered in soft tall grass and I easily waded into my waist with several steps.

"Wow! It's really cold!" I exclaimed to no one in particular.

I took several more steps, turned towards my boys and slowly submerged up to the top of my neck in the frigid water.

It was terrible. It was glorious. It was definitely one of those 6,497 experiences. So I guess I'm down to 6,496 now.

The first few minutes were painful; I was agitated, shivering, and uncomfortable. My wife was taking pictures and videos, asking me if I wanted to share anything. I snapped at her, saying I didn't care about those. And then, something happened. Most likely, the survival centers of my brain released a flood of endorphins, but I'm no neuroscientist, so I'd describe it like this: God emerged. Or maybe that field of indescribable connection, love, meaning, and beauty is always there, and the cold water just cleansed the garbage in the way.

In any case, everything around me came into crystal clear, bright, vivid color. The ripples in the water, the raindrops landing all around me, the blades of grass, the tall trees surrounding the lake. But I'm not just talking about visual acuity and sensory awareness. What I'm talking about is quite hard to describe, but it's something that I know you've felt in your life at the moment of profound risk, challenge, or spiritual clarity.

I became fully, joyfully alive. The discomfort wasn't gone, but it also didn't matter. Everything was beautiful, perfect in its unfolding. I didn't need everything to be easy, or to go my way, or for circumstances to be just so in order to be happy. I was just grateful to be here, to get this time on this mysterious little blue dot.

I looked back at the shore. Both boys stood watching their dad trip out on cold exposure and nature. I could see the urge to get in, and the dread. A battle ensued inside each of them.

It's a battle I know exceedingly well, and I'm sure you do too. The battle between fear and the calling. Between doubt and your destiny. Perhaps that battle is playing out right now in your intimate relationship, your friendships, or your career. You have the desire to do something, go for something, to ultimately be who you really are... But then there's the dread, and the doubt, and the gripping, paralyzing pull to stay on the shore.

I watched my younger son, Arman, who'd initiated this whole experience. I was grateful for his wild, adventurous spirit for initiating this little adventure among hundreds of others.

"This is one of those 'Don't think, just do it moments,'" I called out across the water.

"What?" he shouted back.

"If you want to get in, the more you think about it the harder it will become. To get in you have to command yourself to 'Don't think, just do it!'"

He clenched his little fists several times, took a few deep breaths, and stepped toward the water's edge. Then stopped.

"I can't do it!" he yelled, his voice thick with frustration.

It sure seems that way, doesn't it? I hear this all the time from clients and potential clients. I want to make the changes, I want to liberate myself from social anxiety and niceness, but I just can't take the risks!

Which, of course, is not true. He can get into the water, and you can take the next step towards being more boldly yourself. What's true is that you're scared, and it seems uncomfortable. The rest is the smoke and mirrors of doubt that make a big show about nothing much.

Doubt likes to make itself seem much bigger than the situation really calls for. Much like in cartoons, when the characters are spooked by the shadow of a lion on the cave wall, which turns out to be the oversized shadow of a small cat at the cave entrance.

Doubt puffs itself up to seem mighty and doomfully dangerous. *Don't get into that water —*

you'll die! Don't speak up in that meeting — you'll die! Don't end this relationship — that will kill your partner, and then you'll die of guilt!

The only way out of the hypnotic spell of doubt is to walk through that shadowy cloud of smoke to see what's really on the other side. And all the books, videos, and podcasts in the world are only helpful in that they can give you new perspectives, insight, and courage to actually take the step. But without you taking that step, that's all a bunch of intellectually stimulating smart-person entertainment.

In other words, at some point, my friend, you have to "don't think, just do it!"

I emerged from the lake after about 10 minutes, profoundly changed. I would be back. I knew that for sure. But for now, I needed to warm my core temperature up and began jogging back towards the house.

Arman was tormented. He'd failed to take the courageous step, and now the moment had passed... Or had it?

In the final seconds of opportunity, he turned his gaze back to the silent pond. Defiance, pride, and the universal human spirit welled within him. He didn't say a word, but his body language cried out, "No! I will not die today!"

He marched into the edge of the pond and, without hesitating, dunked his little bony body up to his neck in the water, holding it for a beat, and then popped back up. Frigid, frantic, and most definitely victorious.

My dear friend, I know the mysterious beyond is calling you to share more of who you really are with the world, to boldly speak up and share your ideas at work, thus contributing more to your company or clients, adding more value, and increasing both your income and sense of meaning in your career.

You are called to be more real with those close to you. To be seen and known as you are, rather than posturing, hiding, and pretending to be who you've been taught you're supposed to be.

Ultimately, you are called to take the big risks in your life, the mighty leaps to discover not just what goals you can accomplish but who you are really here to be on this planet and what you're really meant to give.

While I don't know the particulars of your life situation and the next bold step on your path, I do know for certain what that step looks like. It's a bold step into the cold waters of the unknown, right through the looming shadow of doubt. And on the other side, is your version of God, or spiritual freedom, or full, complete, and joyful aliveness. All words for the same thing.

One other thing I know for certain. There is only one time to take that bold step.

And the time is now.

HOW TO
CONNECT WITH ME

Thank you for reading my book. If you are interested in going further with your confidence journey, I would be delighted to support you on that path. There are a number of ways to connect with me and continue your journey toward ever-increasing confidence.

The most impactful way to make rapid changes in your confidence and life is through immersive experiences that help you rapidly reprogram old patterns and upgrade to a new version of you.

Unstoppable Confidence Mastermind

This is an exclusive group program designed to produce radical and rapid transformation in your confidence in all key areas of life. In a deeply supportive community, you'll receive direct coaching and guidance from me and my team through group coaching calls, exclusive workshops, virtual events, daily videos, and so much more.

To learn more, watch inspiring success stories of former members, and apply, visit:

https://www.socialconfidencecenter.com/ucm

Live/Virtual Events

Over the course of three days, you will be immersed in an environment that is inspiring, supportive, and refreshingly authentic. Through dynamic teaching, engaging exercises, and bold action, you will not only learn how to build confidence, you will actually build your confidence muscle real-time at the event.

Live/Virtual events focus on key areas of life, including:

- Conversation Mastery
- Relationship Confidence
- Career & Professional Confidence
- Core Self-Confidence

To find out about upcoming live events with Dr. Aziz, visit: https://www.socialconfidencecenter.com/event

Confidence University

Progress through the most powerful, dynamic, and systematic confidence-building program in the world. You'll make consistent weekly progress through interactive teaching, activities, and Action Steps in the real world. Imagine knowing exactly what to do each day and week to build unstoppable confidence, step-by- step.

https://www.socialconfidencecenter.com/confidenceuniversity

Five Steps to Unleash Your Inner Confidence

This ebook and video mini-course contains powerful and proven techniques used by the world's top psychologists and coaches to help you overcome your fears and self-doubts. Whatever area your lack of confidence is impacting, this ebook can help you. It gives you the basic tools and strategies you need to start mastering your confidence today.

To download your free copy today,

go to www.SocialConfidenceCenter.com

Shrink For The Shy Guy

An in-depth podcast that has hundreds of episodes focused on eliminating social anxiety and awakening your most free, bold, authentic self.

To listen now, go to www.ShrinkForTheShyGuy.com

Get More Confidence YouTube Channel

Hundreds of specific videos guiding you towards greater confidence across all key areas of life.

To watch now, go to www.youtube.com/user/ GetMoreConfidence

ABOUT THE AUTHOR

Dr. Aziz is a psychologist, author, and coach who is internationally known as one of the world's leading experts on confidence. Through his coaching, books, videos, and online media, he has helped thousands of people break through shyness, social anxiety, and self-doubt to create richer, happier, more confident lives.

What is most remarkable about Dr. Aziz is his own personal struggle with self-doubt and social anxiety. After reaching a low point in his own life, he made a powerful decision to do whatever it would take to get the confidence he always wanted. This lead to a passionate pursuit of studying confidence from every source, including books, audio programs, seminars, and a doctorate degree in clinical psychology from Stanford and Palo Alto Universities.

Dr. Aziz is the author of five best-selling books, including *Not Nice* and *The Art of Extraordinary Confidence*, as well as over a dozen e-books, including 5 Steps To Unleash Your Inner Confidence. He is the host of the podcast *Shrink for The Shy Guy* and the YouTube show, *Get More Confidence*. Dr. Aziz is most passionate about his direct work with individuals and groups in coaching programs and weekend seminars.

Dr. Aziz lives in the woods of Oregon with his wife, two boys, and two dogs. To find out more about his personal story and inspiring journey to confidence, visit the "About" section of draziz.com.

Made in the USA
Las Vegas, NV
14 December 2023

82861472R00184